BATTLEFIELDS
THEN & NOW

The sight of the battlefield of Cambrai. From out of the past, the peaceful woodlands of northeast France reveal again the sights of 1917, and the world's first mass tank attack.

BATTLEFIELDS
THEN & NOW

JOHN MAN
TIM NEWARK

MACMILLAN•USA

A QUARTO BOOK

Copyright © 1997 by Quarto Inc

MACMILLAN
A Simon & Schuster Macmillan Company
1633 Broadway
New York, NY 10019-6785

Library of Congress Cataloging-in Publication data
ISBN 0-02-861986-2
Man, John.
Battlefields then & now / John Man & Tim Newark.
p. cm.
Includes index
ISBN 0-02-861986-2
1. Battlefields. 2. Battles. 3. Military history. I. Newark.
Timothy. II. Title.
D25. 5. M36 1997
355.4'09- - dc21   97-15920
CIP

The book was designed and produced by
Quarto Inc.
The Old Brewery
6 Blundell Street
London N7 9BH

EDITORS Anthony Lambert, Tony Hall
SENIOR ART EDITORS Toni Toma, Julie Francis
DESIGNER Malcolm Swanston
ACETATES George Fryer, Kevin Maddison, Tony Gibbons, Terry Hadler
MAPS Peter Gamble, Jonathon Young, Malcolm Swanston
FIGURE ARTWORK Angus McBride
PICTURE RESEARCHER Miriam Hyman
EDITORIAL DIRECTOR Gilly Cameron Cooper
ART DIRECTOR Moira Clinch

Manufactured by Regent Publishing Services Ltd, Hong Kong
Printed by New Island Printing Co. Ltd, Hong Kong

CONTENTS

INTRODUCTION

It seems odd that victory in battle should often depend on the configuration of the landscape. Surely a mastery of tactics and strategy by a great general is more than enough to avoid defeat whatever the location might be? But one has only to read the selection of battles presented in this book to discover that it is the physical shape of a battlefield is often the deciding factor. To understand the nature of a battlefield is to unlock the secrets of victory in war.

The Treacherous Land

Walking across a battlefield is by far the best way to explore the physical realities of past conflicts. Put yourself in the boots of a general and imagine you have to decide on the best place to deploy several thousand soldiers. You look around and immediately begin to size up the extent of high ground, the degree of slope, the presence of any natural obstacles such as clumps of trees or marshy ground, the potential of fortifying a farmhouse or stone wall. This process is exactly that followed by the great commanders of the past, such as Caesar or Napoleon. If you are exploring a battlefield in fine weather, then you are at an advantage, for sometimes commanders had to make these decisions rapidly and in poor light, in rain, or at night. What is more the knowledge that somewhere out there, another army was waiting to destroy their forces simply added to the pressure under which these men worked.

Of course other factors can impede the ideal choice of a battlefield, and can sometimes explain why the greatest commanders failed to make the optimum decisions. In 1815 at Waterloo, for example, Napoleon was under pressure to keep his opponents divided in order to defeat them separately. This compelled him to advance against an army that was protected by the reverse of a slope

In common with many battlefields, Waterloo is visited by thousands each year. The circular white building stands below the Lion Mound and contains a panoramic painting of the battle.

and had fortified a chateau and farmhouses on either flank and in the centre, to defend itself from encirclement and frontal assault. Another crucial factor on this occasion was that the commander of the opposing army was the Duke of Wellington, a general who had perfected the art of selecting a battle ground in order to give his troops the greatest advantage over an attacking force. Wellington's choice of the ground and command of the landscape gave him an edge throughout the day-long combat.

Several battles in the American Civil War show how a treacherous landscape can defeat both greatly superior numbers and generalship. At Antietam in 1862, General Robert E. Lee was caught out by a Northern army almost twice his strength, but by thoroughly understanding the battlefield and making the most of natural obstacles—such as a creek and a sunken road—he managed to inflict such heavy casualties on the opposition that he was left alone to retreat and fight another day. At Gettysburg, on the other hand, it was Lee who was to suffer from an ill-chosen battle ground. Forced into pursuing a Northern army through the town of Gettysburg, he then allowed them to select the high ground outside the town, and thus conduct a defensive battle in which the Confederates threw wave after wave of troops up slopes and across open fields until the very future of the Confederate cause was destroyed by the severe casualties inflicted on it.

Sometimes it is not only the geographical layout of the battlefield, but also the weather conditions on the day of the battle that can make the difference between victory and defeat. At

One of numerous monuments placed on the battlefield of Gettysburg to commemorate a particular action or hero. For example, the Virginia Memorial commemorates the last Confederate assault of the battle, known as "Pickett's Charge" after Major General George E. Pickett who spearheaded the advance of 12,000 Confederate soldiers towards Cemetery Ridge.

Waterloo, heavy rain the night before softened the ground and delayed Napoleon's assault on Wellington's lines. During the First World War, farmland perfectly acceptable for an advance often became an insuperable obstacle because heavy rain and shell fire turned the ground into a quagmire. Mud has often been the arbiter of defeat or victory.

Some of the battles described in this book are sieges, and it would seem that the choice of location was immutable, with the strength of the fortification being the only deciding factor. But here again, the attackers have benefited from an understanding of the geography of the stronghold. The city of Constantinople possessed some of the strongest fortified walls in the medieval world, and it seemed in 1453 that they could resist the assaults of the Turks, just as they had done for hundreds of years. But this time the besiegers understood why the city had survived previous attacks, and by literally transporting a fleet of ships across land, managed to invade the unprotected bay to the north of the city, quickly bringing an end to the siege.

Threat to Command

There are exceptions to the importance of the battlefield in determining the outcome of a contest. Before the twentieth century, commanders used to take a much more active role in leading their men into battle, and were a much more visible presence. This could be turned to the advantage of the boldest general, and sometimes negate the benefit of a superior disposition enjoyed by the enemy. At Gaugamela in 331 BC, Alexander the Great let the Persian king choose the site of battle, even allowing him to remove all obstacles from it so as not to impede the movement of his hordes of chariots and cavalry. However, Alexander knew that the far larger Persian army would stand or fall depending on the performance of their commander; by thrusting his own smaller army directly at the Persian king, he brought the king under pressure, forcing him to flee, and so the Persian army crumbled before him.

The evolution of arms technology has also proved to be a contributing factor to victory or defeat. Although never a substitute for a well-prepared battle ground, sometimes it has enhanced the position of an army. Despite the success in attack of such great commanders such as Napoleon and Alexander the Great, warfare generally favors the defender. In the age of horses and hand-to-hand combat, this might be less decisive, but by the middle of the nineteenth century, military technology had reached a stage of effectiveness that repeating guns and more efficient artillery could lay down such an intense arc of fire that even the bravest, boldest thrust could be annihilated. In this way, General Robert E. Lee on the final day of Gettysburg sent his men forward in a charge of Napoleonic grandeur, only to have them hammered by the power of muskets and concealed artillery before they could reach their objectives.

The military developments in the American Civil War increased in pace and magnitude in the twentieth century, when the aggressive strategy of Germany was brought to a halt in Flanders by a combination of machine guns, long-distance artillery, barbed wire, and trenches. The invention of tanks, armored vehicles, and fighting aircraft returned the advantage to the imaginative attacker in the Second World War, but even then a technological advantage could be defeated by a tenacious defense or, at the very least, could still cost the attacker dearly.

Today, the great victory of the Allied army against the Iraqi's in the Middle Eastern desert suggests that with attack helicopters and guided missiles, we may well be re-entering a new Napoleonic era of bold, sweeping attacks defeating even the most entrenched defender. But the lessons of the war in Vietnam are not so easily swept away by this kind of military revolution, reminding us of the power of poorly armed but highly motivated guerrilla troops using territory they know well to the greatest advantage.

Sacred Land

In surveying the battlefields of yesterday in this book, it is worth remembering that it was not only the fate of nations and generals that were won and lost on these fields. Thousands of ordinary men lost their lives on these battle grounds and in many instances still lie buried in the soil where they fell. These myriad human sacrifices must be recalled as well as the details of tactics and strategy, for they add a spiritual dimension to the geography. In a matter of hours, the lives of thousands of men could be lost; if the battle symbolized a conflict between freedom and tyranny or unity and division, it is a small wonder that these battlefields should be regarded by many nations as sacred ground.

For thousands of years, the lives of those who perished in battle would tend to be forgotten in the chaos of victory and aftermath. Bodies would be stripped of their clothes and valuables and then thrown into a common grave where there would be nothing to mark their individual presence. A man could literally disappear on a battlefield and his family would never know what had happened to him. At Waterloo, over 40,000 men died on all sides, but it was only years later that monuments were erected to their collective memory.

By the middle of the nineteenth century, when warfare had grown even more intense and destructive, there was a general revulsion among civilized populations at this callous treatment of men who had died for nation and beliefs. During the American Civil War, the first large war cemeteries were built in which individual soldiers were marked by headstones in lines. The battlefield at

Gettysburg became a national monument, and in 1864 both Northern and Southern soldiers were buried together on the site of General Robert E. Lee's home on the Potomac River. This later became known as the Arlington National Cemetery, the place of burial for all Americans who served their nation.

In Europe, the great trauma of the First World War and the enormous loss of life prompted the creation of the Commonwealth War Graves Commission. Both British and French govern-ments decided that the bodies of those who died at the front should not be returned home but buried in cemeteries near the site of their deaths. Somber and yet beautiful monuments to the hundreds of thousands of dead were raised all along the Western Front, on battlefields such as the Somme, and their simple rows of white head-stones are still an unforgettable and moving memorial to the tragic loss of war. Ever since then, it has become the custom to raise monu-ments and remember the dead of battle at the place they died, and many organizations have fought long and hard to extend this act of remem-brance to battlefields further back in history. Many of the battlefields described in this book have been preserved and honored in this way, and can be visited today as a vivid reminder of past combat and sacrifice.

Some of the strongest defenses in the medieval world were overcome by the ingenious use of the terrain: Constantinople fell after ships were taken overland to outflank its fortifications.

GAUGAMELA 331 B.C.

The battle that sealed the fate of the Persian empire was won by the military genius of Alexander the Great. He conquered unprecedented swathes of territory in battles that involved hundreds of thousands of troops and charioteers.

Alexander the Great had the spirit of a conquistador. He had ambition without bounds, without frontiers. When he stood on the edge of a continent with his army and determined to take it, he was on the point of destroying one of the oldest empires in the world.

The Greatest Campaign

Alexander learned his ambition from his father, Philip of Macedon. He also learned from him a highly effective kind of warfare. When Philip descended from the mountains of Macedonia, he took on the martial states of Greece—warrior cultures that had defeated a Persian invasion. Their strength was based on the phalanx, a group of soldiers—each armed with a shield and long spear—moving as one body. Philip added to this the flexibility and speed of horsemen armed with swords and spears. By using both forms of fighting units, he overwhelmed the city-states and made himself master of Greece. Alexander served with his father as a cavalryman and saw the effectiveness of the Macedonian fighting force at first hand. He was eager to try it out elsewhere. He believed his father no longer had the will to conquer and accused him as he stumbled, happily drunk, at a party: "There is a man who wants to move from continent to continent and cannot even walk from chair to chair." A short time later, Philip was assassinated and Alexander inherited his army.

In 334 B.C., Alexander embarked on one of the greatest campaigns ever fought in the history of the world. It would take him from Greece to the jungles of India, to the deserts of Central Asia, and the sumptuous splendor of Babylon. But all this belonged to the Persian empire, a massive construct of nations similar in apparent power and influence to that of the Soviet Union at the height of the Cold War. Its emperor, Darius, could call upon tens of thousands of warriors from all corners of his dominion. When he first heard of Alexander's appearance, he must have considered it a presumptuous raid, to be swept away like a fly. In the battle of Granicus, Alexander proved he could not be so easily swatted. A year later, Darius decided to confront this impudent barbarian himself at the Battle of Issus. Again, Alexander overturned the numerical superiority of the emperor and hounded him from the field.

Bronze figure of an ancient Greek hoplite warrior, fifth century B.C. Warriors such as this, armed with shield, spear, and sword, were at the core of Alexander's conquering army. The figure is now in the Berlin Museum of Antiquities.

Bodyguard of the Persian kings, from a frieze at the citadel of Susa. These warriors, known as the Immortals, were the elite of the Persian army, but not even they could save Darius from the ferocity of Alexander's onslaught.

The situation was now critical. If Alexander was allowed to continue his defiance, then all the kings who owed Darius allegiance would wonder who was in charge and his empire would crumble. Darius had to stop Alexander once and for all. There would be no further chances.

The Final Contest

In 331 B.C., Alexander advanced from Syria into the heartland of the Persian empire in Mesopotamia, present-day Iraq. His target was Babylon, and on a plain between the ancient towns of Arbela and Gaugamela, Alexander ran into the might of Darius. The Persian force was said to amount to some 200,000 troops, though this is probably an exaggeration; nonetheless Darius's array of soldiers was impressive. Around him stood his elite Persian bodyguard. On either side of them were Greek mercenaries who fought in the same phalanx style as the Macedonians. On his left flank was a thunderous mass of horsemen from Central Asia, Turkish peoples who fought with bow and arrow. In front of these were a hun-

dred chariots with scythes attached to their wheels. On his right flank was another mass of horsemen, this time including Parthians and Medes, renowned for their archery. Finally, on top of this, came a group of war elephants—the ancient equivalent of the tank—from India.

Alexander's army numbered some 40,000 foot-soldiers and 7,000 horsemen, but these were veteran warriors who believed that Alexander was almost a god who could not be defeated. That said, on the morning of the battle, Alexander's officers possessed a natural anxiety and were shocked to find their leader still sleeping in his tent as though it was the morning after the battle. Darius had chosen the battlefield, having realized that his previous two defeats had been due in part to rough terrain that broke up the movement of his troops. This time, he wanted the majestic sweep of his chariots to be unhindered so he had slaves remove all the bushes and natural obstacles from the field. His confidence rose as he pictured the tiny Macedonian force before him.

Alexander rode at the head of his elite loyal cavalry, called "Companions." These formed his

Greek bronze helmet of the Corinthian style, fifth century B.C. Warriors in the crush of battle stood as much chance of being wounded by the weapons of their comrades as by the enemy.

A detail from a picture painted 1,933 years after the battle of Gaugamela, in 1602, by the Dutch painter Pieter Brueghel (1568–1625).

right flank and were placed ahead of the other troops in what is known as an echelon or slanted formation. Behind these horsemen and in the center was the mighty Macedonian phalanx, a solid core of spear-wielding footsoldiers around which his other formations could move. Behind them and on the left flank were the rest of his Greek cavalry. Knowing that Darius's army vastly outnumbered his own, Alexander took a further precaution and added reserve units behind each flank to protect them from encirclement. It was an aggressive method of battle, but one which also took sensible defensive precautions.

Without being able to rely on a mastery of the terrain, Alexander would have to depend on that other great battle winner—a direct strike at the enemy commander. That was far easier said than done, and in an almost mocking opening move, Darius sent forward his hundred war chariots.

Thundering across the plain, the myriad horses and spiked wheels kicked up a massive cloud of dust. Many lesser armies would have fled at this awesome sight, but Alexander's light infantry, armed with javelins and bows, pelted the horses, throwing them into confusion so that by the time they confronted the main Greek formations, their

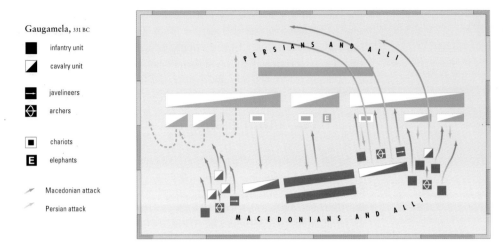

Gaugamela, 331 BC

- ◼ infantry unit
- ◤ cavalry unit
- ⊟ javelineers
- ⊕ archers
- ◼ chariots
- E elephants
- ⟋ Macedonian attack
- ⟋ Persian attack

impetus had been lost and they could do nothing but save their lives and rattle back. Alexander then spurred his horse forward and the Companions made a dash toward the Persian lines. Persian and Turkish horsemen swept forward to meet him, impatient for a fight, and naturally rode to the flank of the Macedonians, hoping to encircle them. But Alexander's reserves countered this move, allowing the Companions to crash into the Persian center. Similarly, on Alexander's left flank, the bow-

Persian chariot and cavalry bristling with archers. Darius sought to overwhelm Alexander with his mass of chariots at the beginning of the battle, but Alexander weakened their impact with infantry.

carrying Persian horsemen swept around in a pincer movement, but his reserves anticipated this and held them in fierce fighting.

Alexander had guessed correctly and now personally led a ferocious fight on a center weakened by the departure of the horsemen to his flank. His Macedonian phalanx caught up with him and literally smashed into the soldiers surrounding Darius—their long spears piercing and splintering the emperor's bodyguard, impaling troops, and thrusting them back on their comrades. It was a vicious way of fighting, and the Macedonians were practiced in it. The Greek mercenaries fought back in a like manner with their long spears, but as mercenaries they possessed no loyalty to the emperor. As Alexander piled on the pressure, Darius decided he had had enough. He ordered his royal chariot to turn around and fled the field while his army disintegrated before Alexander's cavalry and spearmen. It was Darius's last chance to hang on to his empire. A year later, he was to be found dead beside a road, killed by his own desperate supporters. Alexander was now master of the Persian empire. He marched into Babylon, with riches and greetings for the new emperor.

ALEXANDER THE GOD

As Alexander advanced through an ancient world of which he was becoming increasingly its master, it is not surprising that he should think himself a god. Such power and success would make anyone feel supreme, but it was not simply a question of feeling like a god—Alexander considered himself in reality a god.

Military command in the ancient world was very much a personal factor. A man—or sometimes a woman—could personally take command of an army, ride at its head, and lead it into battle. An army thrived or declined on the personal strength of its leader. Alexander understood this perfectly, and as a result could lead his men anywhere and achieve the most remarkable victories against almost impossible odds. Alexander encouraged loyalty and reverence by associating himself with the gods.

When Alexander took his first steps on the Asian continent, he immediately led his warriors to the town of Troy, the legendary site of that great epic of Greek literature, the *Iliad*. Here, semi-divine Greek warriors had fought a long and heroic siege against the Trojans. Alexander believed that he was descended from the Greek hero Achilles, so he made sacrifices at his tomb. But Alexander had an even greater vision of his own divinity: When Alexander chose to have his image immortalized on coins, he was portrayed with horns, the sign of the god Dionysus. Dionysus was the wild god, the god of the impetuous, violent spirit that lurks inside men and women and is liberated by alcohol. A son of Zeus, he left his homeland to roam across the world accompanied by a wild army of satyrs and maenads, spreading the use of wine, conquering armies in Egypt and Asia, and marching as far afield as India. Here was a model for Alexander's ambition and a sign that the way he lived could lead to remarkable conquests. Even his passion for alcohol was central to this, chroniclers tell of his wild drinking sessions in which even his friends sometimes fell victim to his violence .

In Egypt, Alexander's understanding of himself as a god was strengthened by leading an expedition into the desert to visit the temple of Ammon. As he approached the temple, the Egyptian priests recognized him as the son of Ammon, the supreme Egyptian god, equivalent to the Greek Zeus.

Here again, Alexander was recognized as the son of Zeus, just like Dionysus. Plutarch, an ancient historian of Alexander, explains this by saying "Alexander did not allow himself to become vain or foolishly conceited because of his belief in his divinity, but rather used it to assert his authority over others." This may well be true, but there can be little doubt that Alexander believed he was the god Dionysus.

Floor mosaic of Darius, in the chariot, defeated by Alexander the Great at the Battle of Issus.

ALESIA 52 B.C.

Few battles have had such a bizarre disposition of opposing forces as Alesia, where the Romans besieging a Celtic hillfort were themselves surrounded by allies of the Celts. The Roman defenses, though hastily built, were crucial in securing victory.

Julius Caesar (102-44 B.C.), as recorded by a bust in the British Museum. Few generals can rival Caesar for the brilliance with which he fought numerous campaigns. Though he exercised the power of a dictator, Caesar was a polymath who ruled with a degree of benevolence and enlightenment rare for his times. His conspiratorial assassination by a group of aristocrats was intended to prevent the emergence of a hereditary monarchy.

Like many later politicians, Julius Caesar realized that one of the best routes to political power was a successful military career. Accordingly, as a young man, he placed himself in the forefront of the border wars with the Celts. His first military experience was won against the Celts in Spain, but his eyes were on the biggest Celtic prize of all—the rich lands of Gaul, the ancient name for France.

Divide and Conquer

Unlike Alexander the Great, who considered himself a god and trusted his divine power to bring him victory in battle, Caesar was a far more practical man. He understood the precarious nature of events. "Fortune," he wrote, "which has great influence on affairs generally and especially in war, produces by a slight disturbance of balance important changes in human affairs."

Knowing this, Caesar did everything to prepare his ground for a campaign, and that included political preparation. When he first invaded Gaul, he made sure it was in response to a plea from a Celtic tribe for help against invading Germans. Appearing as a savior rather than an invader, Caesar thus advanced further into Gaul and managed to have Celts fight on his side against other Celtic tribes with which they had disputes. Through the principle of divide and conquer, Caesar quickly found himself master of Gaul, but not all Celts were so easily misled; in central France, Caesar was forced to confront a Gallic leader of comparable military and political skills.

Vercingetorix was chieftain of the Averni, a Celtic tribe living in the centre of France. A powerful personality, Vercingetorix instilled a strict discipline into his warriors. Neighboring tribes were asked to submit hostages to him, and disaffection was punished with death. So far, Caesar had restricted his invasion of Gaul to securing a ring of conquered strongholds around central Gaul, but the defiance of the Averni invited him into the interior.

Caesar tracked down the Celts to a hillfort at Gergovia, the capital of the Averni. In his assault on the fort, Caesar depended on his tried-and-true system of Roman legionaries battling alongside allied Celtic cavalry, but this time it all went wrong. His Roman soldiers were surprised by the arrival of their own Gallic cavalry who looked identical to the enemy's Celtic horsemen. According to Caesar, friendly troops usually "left their right shoulders uncovered as an agreed sign," but clearly this did not happen. It may have been the hand of Vercingetorix at work to create confusion on the battlefield. Whatever the reason, the Romans were savagely beaten and forced away from the hillfort. The result was catastrophic for Caesar's political mastery. His aura of invincibility was broken and Celtic tribes throughout Gaul joined Vercingetorix. Even Caesar's most loyal Gallic supporters, the Aedui, threw in their lot with the Averni.

Rather than fleeing this challenge, Caesar methodically set about reconstructing and

A Roman soldier carries the characteristic eagle standard of the Roman army. Made in the first century A.D., the bronze figurine is now in the Alba Fucene in Rome.

The site of Alesia today near the village of Alise-Ste-Reine, clearly an impressive position for a Celtic hill-fort with rivers running on either side of the main mound.

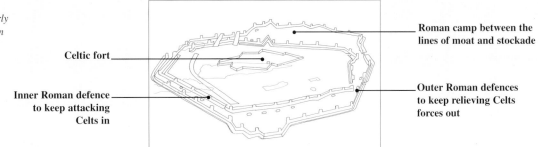

Roman camp between the lines of moat and stockade

Celtic fort

Inner Roman defence to keep attacking Celts in

Outer Roman defences to keep relieving Celts forces out

strengthening his army. He invited the Germans, traditional enemies of the Gauls, to supply him with friendly cavalry. He then went after Vercingetorix, knowing, like Alexander, that he was the key to the whole campaign. Caesar found the Gallic chieftain in the hilltop fort of Alesia, an awesome rocky plateau known today as Mont-Auxois, some 30 miles (48 km) west of Dijon in Burgundy. Surrounded by steep river valleys on three sides within a fortress of wooden palisades and earth slopes with tens of thousands of troops at his side, Vercingetorix was in no hurry to meet the Roman warlord. He would wait for an army of Gallic reinforcements to join him, and together they would crush the Roman adventurer.

Roman Logic

With Vercingetorix trapped inside an impregnable fortress, Caesar now embarked on an endeavour which only a Roman of Caesar's logical determi-

nation would consider worthwhile. Caesar had an army of almost 50,000 to call upon, including ten legions of Roman soldiers, several thousand barbarian cavalry, and numerous camp followers. Rather than order a pointless attack on the hill-fort, as a lesser tyrant might have done, Caesar told them to start digging. This enormous workforce set about creating a ring of fortifications around the hill-fort. It was a gigantic task. A ditch 8 feet (2.5 meters) deep and 15 feet (4.5 meters) wide was dug in an 11-mile- (17.6 km-) long ring around Alesia. The earth from the ditch was piled behind it, and on top of this mound was raised a wooden barricade with the addition of 23 small forts built at regular intervals around the circle.

Surprised at the thoroughness of the endeavor, Vercingetorix realized he had sufficient food and stores to survive only a month-long siege. Before the ring of forts was fully completed, he hastily sent out a troop of horsemen to insist on his allies coming to his rescue. But Caesar was one step

Right: *Reconstruction showing the Romans building the great wooden towers that formed the heart of Caesar's ring of fortifications. To the bottom left is a ballista, a spear-hurling piece of artillery much favored by the Romans.*

Below: *Reconstruction of the fortified wall built by Julius Caesar to surround the Celtic hill-fort. The defenses serve to break up an advance on foot or horseback.*

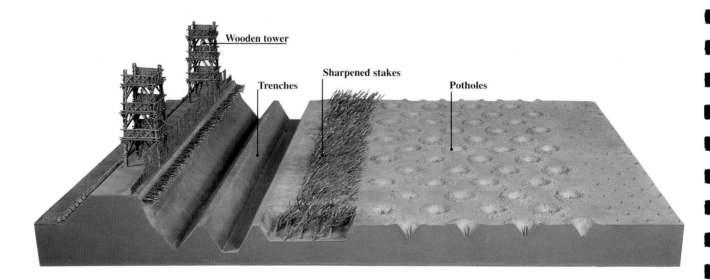

Wooden tower

Trenches

Sharpened stakes

Potholes

ahead of him. Knowing that a relieving army could assault him from behind his fortifications, Caesar then ordered his men to build a second, even bigger ring of defenses to protect his rear, thus creating a fortress around a fortress. To this he had further trenches dug, some filled with sharpened stakes and others flooded with water from the nearby rivers. It was a monumental achievement. But it was also good sense, for Vercingetorix's call for help did not go unanswered. Some 43 tribes from Gaul sent him tens of thousands of warriors and this mighty horde marched on Caesar's encampment.

The strength of a Celtic army was its cavalry, which was made up of some of the finest horse-men in the ancient world. They fought with spears flung from horseback and long swords to cut down footsoldiers. The Romans had employed them for centuries as mercenaries, and Caesar knew that he had to confront this menace outside his ring of defenses. Watched from the battlements of the fortifications, thousands of cavalry now clashed in a major battle on the plain just beneath the hillfort. It was a vicious confrontation fueled by ethnic hatred, as Caesar's German cavalry fought Celts. Despite being out-numbered, the Germans finally rallied and charged the relieving force of Celts, throwing them back on to their camp. Having failed to crush the Romans in an open battle, the Celts now turned to subterfuge. Under the cover of night, Celtic warriors carried bundles of sticks, ladders, and grappling hooks toward the outer ring of for-tifications. Throwing the bundles into the trench-es, they now rushed over them and propped their ladders against the barricades. The Roman guards shouted the alert, and soon they were battling with the Gauls to keep them off the barricades, employing artillery such as the ballista, a massive spear-throwing device. The shouts of attack encouraged Vercingetorix to join the assault from his side and attack the inner ring, which severely stretched the Roman defenses. But the darkness created confusion, and many Celts fell into the stake- and water-filled trenches. Despite being

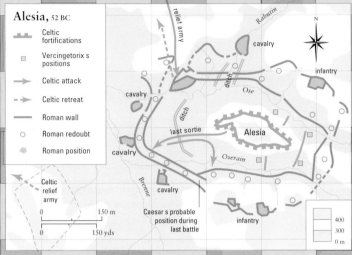

Roman soldiers portrayed on a Roman mosaic of the 1st–2nd century A.D. It is a rather fanciful interpretation, and certainly Caesar's soldiers would have worn coats of mail armor.

attacked on both fronts, Caesar's men kept a solid guard on the battlements, preventing any breakthrough of the two forces. By dawn, the Celts attacking the outer ring were exhausted and feared a counterattack. They retreated to their camp, and Vercingetorix returned to his hillfort. Caesar's painstaking preparation had paid off, and the situation looked grim for Vercingetorix.

The Celts outside the fortifications now looked upon the problem tactically. Rather than risking another frontal assault from the plain, they sent out scouts to inspect the whole extent of Caesar's

defenses. Around the other side of the hillfort in the rough terrain of the valleys, the ring of forts was at its weakest. It was now time to test the resolve of the Romans. A major force of Celts was sent through the night to arrive at the far end of the fortifications. Screaming and yelling their defiance, they rushed upon the barricades, using bundles of sticks and ladders to ease their assault. Caesar quickly reacted to this, but as he did so the Celts launched another attack from the plain, and, as before, Vercingetorix joined in also from inside the hill-fort. Caesar now had to confront three major attacks at different points on his fortifications and his army was spread very thinly. There was fighting everywhere, and Caesar had to ride from point to point, using his reserves judiciously only when the defenses were actually breached. It was at this moment that his personal leadership mattered most and—wearing a red cloak—his troops could see that he was personally fighting alongside his hard-pressed men.

At some points the barricade was physically pulled down, but again and again, Caesar plugged these gaps with his reserves. Caesar, in his recollections of the campaign, described the desperate nature of the combat: "Both sides realized that this was the time, above all others, for a supreme effort. The Gauls knew that unless they broke through the lines they were totally lost. The Romans, if they held their ground, could look forward to the end of all their hardships."

By the late afternoon, the sheer weight of numbers was beginning to tell. Celts attacking from the plain had breached the Roman ramparts and were surging over the broken barricades. Caesar now had just one choice. He had either to withdraw behind his fortifications or renew the impetus with an attack. Leading a combination of cavalry and foot soldiers, he broke out of the crush and led them round to attack the Celts in the rear. Panic broke out as some Celts wondered whether this was a completely new Roman army. There was great slaughter, and Caesar finally broke the will of the relieving army. Vercingetorix had had enough. He recalled his men to the hillfort while German cavalry men chased Celtic stragglers deep into the forest.

Inside Alesia, Vercingetorix realized any hope of securing victory was gone. By allowing Caesar to bottle him up in his hillfort, he had let his enormous support be divided. Disillusioned and without any further ideas, he turned to his supporters and let them decide his fate. They could either kill him now or hand him over to the Romans. None of the Celts would make the decision and instead a messenger was sent out to Caesar. It was up to the Roman to decide.

Savoring his moment of victory, Caesar erected a large platform outside the hillfort on which he sat with his officers. The rebel chieftains were to parade before him and lay down their arms. Vercingetorix was the last to leave the hillfort. Wearing his finest armor, he rode out on a beautiful horse. In front of Caesar, he slid off his horse, removed his armor, and kneeled motionless before the Roman. All Celtic resistance in Gaul was over. Caesar had conquered a new land and he would return to Rome in triumph with Vercingetorix in chains. The stage was now set for Caesar to claim political power in Rome.

Today, the tiny village of Alise-Ste-Reine is perched on the edge of the plateau that once held the Celtic hilltop fort. In the nineteenth century, Napoleon III, Emperor of France, was so taken by this story of Gallic defiance that he had the ground dug up over the battlefield and uncovered a number of weapons and bones. To honor the memory of Vercingetorix, he had a giant statue erected depicting him as an impressive figure with long hair and a full moustache. On the base of the statue a statement attributed to the Celtic warlord is engraved: "A single and united Gaul, all of the same mind, can defy the universe." It was a lesson that Napoleon III did not want forgotten. The statue still stands on the battlefield overlooking the plain where the most intense fighting took place.

Roman soldiers forming the testudo, in which shields are carried above their heads to protect them when assaulting a fort. The scene is taken from the Column of Marcus Aurelius, portraying a campaign against German tribesmen in the 2nd century A.D.

CELTIC HORSEMANSHIP

The Celts were renowned as great horsemen in the ancient world. Their cavalries were employed by both the Greeks and Romans, and they served under the greatest military commanders, including Caesar and Hannibal.

An early description exists of their fighting prowess against the Thebans, which was written by the Greek soldier Xenophon. "Few though they were," he wrote, "they were scattered here and there. They charged towards the Thebans, threw their javelins, and then dashed away as the enemy moved towards them, often turning and throwing more javelins. While pursuing these tactics, they sometimes dismounted for a rest. But if anyone charged upon them while they were resting, they would easily leap onto their horses and retreat. If enemy warriors pursued them far from the Theban army, these horsemen would then turn around and stab them with their javelins. Thus they manipulated the entire Theban army, compelling it to advance or fall back at their will."

HASTINGS 1066

One of Europe's most famous battles dramatically altered the course of English history when the Norman victors ended centuries of Saxon rule. The outcome of the evenly matched struggle was largely determined by a stroke of luck for William.

William of Normandy or William I of England (1027–87) was the illegitimate son of Robert III, Duke of Normandy. William was nonetheless accepted as duke on his father's death in 1035. In 1051 he visited his cousin King Edward the Confessor in England and was promised the throne. On Edward's death, however, Harold became king.

If ever a kingdom, if ever a nation was lost in one day, then it was Saxon England on the field of Hastings in 1066. William, Duke of Normandy, claimed that Edward, King of England, had promised that he would succeed to the English throne. When Edward's brother-in-law, Harold Godwinson, ignored William's claim and assumed the throne himself in 1066, a confrontation was inevitable.

Poised to Fight

Harold was the dominant figure in England, the power behind the throne during Edward's reign. He could call on a formidable army of Saxon warriors. William was his equal in northern France, having recently crushed a rebellion in Brittany. His Norman knights were the leading warriors of their day, equipped with mail armor and fighting from horseback with lance and sword. The descendants of northern invaders, they had Viking blood in them.

The steps towards confrontation began in the summer of 1066. William had a huge fleet built to transport his warriors, horses, and supporters across the English Channel. Meanwhile, Harold had to secure his position in England against not only William's rumored invasion, but also against the threats of other warlords hungry for the English throne. In September, a Norwegian army landed on the coast of Northumbria in the north of England, and crushed a Saxon army marching into York. Harold responded quickly and con-

fronted the invaders at the Battle of Stamford Bridge. The Norwegian army broke and their leaders were slain. Harold could claim a great victory, but as his men celebrated, word reached them that William had launched an invasion of southern England.

Too Tired for Victory?

It has often been argued that it was the hasty march south forced on Harold and his men that undermined their ability to fight at Hastings; having marched over 200 miles (322 km) in something like a week, they were simply too exhausted to maintain a full day's battle against the Normans. Such an interpretation, however, is based on our own modern view of physical endurance. Harold's Saxon warriors were a different breed. With spirits uplifted both by victory and loot, Harold's lightly equipped army could easily have covered the ground. (Such sturdiness is not impossible to find today: the photo-journalist Ken Guest has compared Harold's soldiers to the hardy peasant warriors he worked with in Afghanistan during that country's war with Russia. These men were accustomed to walking 12 hours a day over some of the world's harshest mountain terrain, stopping only briefly for prayers or tea.)

The Saxon and Norman armies finally met on October 14 on a hillside some 8 miles (13 km) north of the modern town of Hastings in Sussex (southern England). Harold knew the land well

Harold II (c.1022–66), with a hawk on his arm, was Earl Godwin's second son. As Edward's righthand man, Harold displayed great abilities as well as being an able soldier.

MAR E

and chose a strong defensive position on top of a ridge, with the forest protecting his flanks and with marshy ground in front of him. William had no other choice but to launch a frontal assault. Harold ordered those soldiers on horseback to dismount and to form a shield-wall with the foot-soldiers. They could in this way protect themselves from arrows and make themselves less vulnerable to breaks in their own line.

The Rivals Clash

We do not know the numbers of troops involved on that day of battle. It has been suggested that each army was around 8,000 men strong; certainly, Dark Age armies were not great in numbers. What we do know is that William organized his invading army into three large groups: loyal Norman warriors at the center, French allies on his right flank, and Breton allies to the left. Within these groups, archers stood at the front, footsoldiers in the middle, and armored horsemen at the rear. On the face of it, William was at a disadvantage. He had lost the opportunity to prepare his ground by allowing the Saxons to dictate the site of the battle; he was attacking uphill with little possibility of turning his opponent's flanks. In contrast, the Saxons had the stronger motivation, having just won a victory under their dynamic leader and were defending their homeland.

Although the circumstances for an attack were far from ideal, William clearly trusted his

A ship of William's fleet sails across the English Channel loaded with warriors and their horses. Detail from the Bayeux Tapestry.

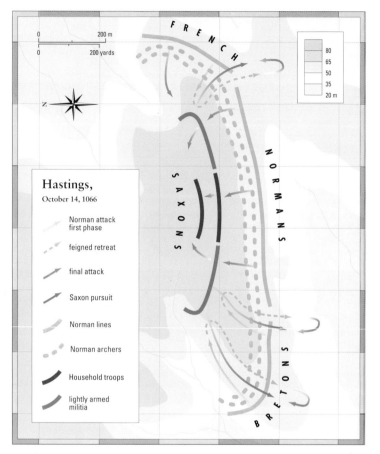

Hastings,
October 14, 1066

Norman attack
first phase

feigned retreat

final attack

Saxon pursuit

Norman lines

Norman archers

Household troops

lightly armed
militia

Harold. This is where the preparations of the last seven months had been leading, and he had nowhere to hide in an alien land. The fight began at 9 A.M. William's soldiers advanced up the slope to the ridge. His archers laid down a shower of arrows, but this was matched by more arrows, stones, and javelins flung from behind the Saxon shield-wall. The two sides clashed: Saxon swords rang against Breton blades; William's horsemen thrust their lances between Harold's shields; and Viking axes severed Norman armor. In this first onslaught, both sides gave their greatest effort, hoping to win through sheer ferocity and energy. As the two lines flexed and wavered on the brink of victory or defeat, it was the Bretons who first broke. As they ran back down the hill, chased by the Saxons, the cry went up that William himself had been killed and the battle was over.

William acted swiftly to halt his army's collapse. He removed his helmet and waved it, riding among his men to show that he was still alive. This was the crisis point of the battle and William was resolute in maintaining his men's morale. Sword in hand, he led a countercharge that rallied his troops behind him. Some of the Saxons who had been pursuing the fleeing Bretons were surrounded and slaughtered, but the majority of Harold's warriors returned to their position and the fighting continued.

Interpretations of what followed vary. William of Poitiers, a Norman retainer and later a chronicler of the battle, claimed that William then ordered a series of feigned retreats to tempt more troops from Harold's line—no doubt after having noted the success of his horsemen against the eagerly pursuing Saxons. This may have been the case; certainly Harold's tired but confident warriors would have been eager to follow up any apparent weakness, but it also sounds like the attempt of a loyal courtier to make William seem like a greater general than he was in this conflict. Feigned retreats are enormously difficult to carry

warriors and their fighting powers. Norman knights were nothing less than professional killing machines, clad from head to foot in thick mail armor and ready to hurl or thrust their deadly lances at the enemy. Harold, however, was no more poorly served by his soldiers. Surrounding him on the ridge at Hastings were his elite bodyguard of huscarls, fierce armored warriors loyal until death. Many of them fought with great two-handed battle-axes, a weapon that could strike a man dead with one blow and cleave great gaps in any battle group.

Despite any misgivings he might have as a commander, William had little choice but to attack out in the heat of battle and can all too often turn into a real rout. It is difficult to believe that William's army, in an already precarious situation, with the steadfastness of its non-Norman contingents in doubt, could really have carried out these retreats successfully.

It is more likely that these attacks were akin to raids on the Saxon line. By this point both sides must have been completely exhausted, drained by their enormous exertion and the stress of combat—a situation where one-off raids would have been more likely than risky maneuvers. Whatever the reality of William's tactics, however, they appear to have had little effect on Harold's resolve. Still, he stood on the ridge and defied his enemy on the slope below. In that lay the key to the whole struggle.

A Single Arrow

All armies, at all times, depend on the knowledge that their commanders are in charge. Whether they are actually present on the battlefield or are viewed before the combat begins, it raises the spirit of each man to know that his commander shares his fate. If the commander is killed or leaves the battlefield, then the battle is more likely to be lost from that moment on. This was never more true than in medieval warfare, when a commander physically stood in line with his warriors.

As the day passed and the threat of his army disintegrating drew nearer, William launched one final great attack. All his troops charged up the hill. His archers laid down a dense blizzard of arrows, and his men, knowing that retreat meant a dismal, deadly hunt through alien land, fought with a desperate vigor. It was in this final clash that William's luck came through. A single arrow flew over the Saxon shields and plunged into Harold's eye. As the great warlord struggled to remove it, the wall of iron around him faltered. Norman knights broke into the throng of his

Norman cavalry continue to harass the Saxon shield-wall, throwing javelins at the dismounted Saxons. Detail from the Bayeux Tapestry.

bodyguards, and Harold was cut to the ground. With this one incident, the battle was won and lost. Both sides had fought each other almost to a standstill. Neither side lacked in courage or martial skill. Harold had created for himself an edge over William by choosing his position, but not even his good generalship could overturn the simple fact of his own death. As the fatal news spread, the retreat began, degenerating into a rout as Norman horsemen hunted the fleeing warriors. It was a fate that only hours before they had feared for themselves.

After a day when luck played such a key role, it is not surprising that William gave thanks to God. He ordered that an abbey be built on the site of the battle, the ruins of which can still be seen today. Legend has it that the altar was situated on the spot where Harold fell. William did not delay in taking advantage of his good fortune and quickly marched on London where he assumed the crown of England. That such a prize should be won in just one battle may seem surprising, but the fate of the Saxon dynasty was very much bound up with the fate of Harold. When he ceased to exist, so did much resistance to what many might well have viewed as just another invasion of the northmen, which had to be endured and absorbed over time.

CONSTANTINOPLE 1453

Few battles have had such a profound effect on subsequent history as the fall of Constantinople and the death of the last Roman emperor. Nor has such ingenuity been used to overcome defenses that had withstood assaults for a thousand years.

Mehmet II, Turkish sultan and conqueror of Constantinople. This portrait of him, attributed to Sinan Bey, c.1475, is now in the Topkapi Palace Museum, Istanbul.

Constantinople was considered the second Rome. When the ancient city of Rome fell to the barbarians in the fifth century, it was to the city of Constantinople that everyone looked to maintain the jewel of civilization that was known as the Roman Empire.

Mighty Walls of God

It was in Constantinople that a Roman Emperor still ruled, long after the last emperor in Rome had been assassinated. It was also here that the biggest church in Christendom was raised—St. Sophia, its vast dome decorated with glittering golden mosaics. As the centuries passed, the reputation of Constantinople grew with its riches, made from the myriad merchants traveling between Europe and Asia. Everyone had to pass through Constantinople, for it stood on the tip of eastern Europe, commanding the Bosporous, the strip of water dividing Asia from Europe and joining the Mediterranean and Black seas. That such a city should be conquered was unthinkable.

For a thousand years, Constantinople resisted the assault of barbarians and foreign armies. First built in the fifth century, its gigantic walls were preceded by a moat 60 feet (18 meters) wide and 30 feet (9 meters) deep. Behind this came a wall about 30 feet high and 7 feet (2 meters) thick, its 96 towers placed at regular intervals covering the western land side of the city and its two sea sides, the city being roughly triangular in shape. Behind these outer walls was an even bigger defense,

walls that were 16 feet (5 meters) thick and 40 feet (12 meters) high, again with 96 towers. When Attila the Hun rode up to the city in the fifth century with his horde of barbarians, he thought better of the task and moved on to an easier target. It is little wonder that many people considered the city to be protected by God himself.

By the fifteenth century, the power of the Roman or Byzantine (so called because they spoke Greek rather than Latin) emperors living within Constantinople was in serious decline. A new force of Ottoman Turks had advanced out of central Asia, conquered all their Asian realm, and crossed the Bosporous into Europe, where they gobbled up territory in the Balkans. Yet even these Turks had thought better of attacking the great walls and had left Constantinople to become a Christian island in a Muslim sea. Until, that is, Mehmet, the son of a slave-girl and the sultan, thought the unthinkable and recommended the conquest of this last Christian bastion. His father thought the idea was crazy, but when he died and his son Mehmet became sultan at only 21, his foremost ambition was to be remembered as the warrior who brought a thousand years of Roman history to an end.

Mehmet prepared his campaign carefully, and in 1452 he had a castle built on the European side of the Bosporous, just north of the great city. This castle, called Rumeli Hisar, still stands today and is remarkable for having been built in months rather than years. After the emperor of Constantinople, a Greek called Constantine XI,

Mehmet II enters Constantinople in 1453 surrounded by his Ottoman soldiers, in this sixteenth-century miniature.

Section of the city walls that withstood the 1453 bombardment.

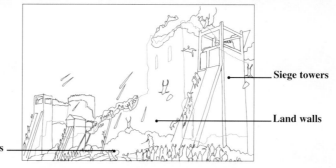

Siege towers

Land walls

Specially made siege guns

protested at this trespass on his land, Mehmet had his ambassadors executed. The meaning was clear, and Constantine sent messages to Italy asking the Pope and the Venetians to come to his assistance with a crusader army. In the meantime, he had the walls reinforced and his people prepare for a siege, gathering food and filling the great underground cisterns with water.

But all that came from Italy was a handful of ships bringing a few hundred Italian troops to protect the commercial interests of merchants based in the city. By 1453, the total defense force

numbered only some 8,000 men, the majority being Greeks of the Imperial Guard or men raised from the city; the rest were Italian mercenaries or sailors and merchants from Genoa and Venice.

By spring, the Ottoman Turkish army was approximately 160,000 strong, outnumbering the defenders twenty to one. The Turkish army consisted of both Turkish and European soldiers, many recruited from the Balkans, the finest being called Janissaries—European slaves raised as devout Muslims who fought fiercely and faithfully for the sultan. In addition to these elite war-

riors, the sultan had brought together a fleet of some 90 warships as well as 200 cannon. The artillery was the pride and joy of Mehmet's army. The use of cannons had increased as their efficiency improved. For this siege, Mehmet had a giant cannon cast out of 8-inch-thick (20-cm) bronze, with a barrel nearly 27 feet (8 meters)

Constantinople from a picture published in 1520. On the right is the Golden Horn, the long bay protected by a chain. At the bottom is the palace of the sultan built on the remains of the palace belonging to the last Byzantine emperor.

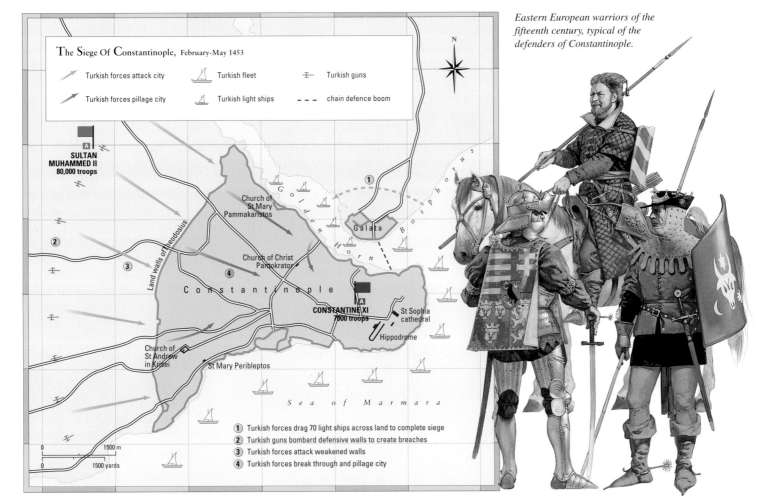

Eastern European warriors of the fifteenth century, typical of the defenders of Constantinople.

The Siege Of Constantinople, February–May 1453

Turkish forces attack city	Turkish fleet	Turkish guns
Turkish forces pillage city	Turkish light ships	chain defence boom

SULTAN
MUHAMMED II
80,000 troops

Church of
St Mary
Pammakaristos

Galata

Land walls of Theodosius

Church of Christ
Pantokrator

C o n s t a n t i n o p l e

CONSTANTINE XI
7000 troops

St Sophia
cathedral

Hippodrome

Church of
St Andrew
in Krisei

St Mary Peribleptos

G o l d e n   H o r n

B o s p h o r u s

S e a   o f   M a r m a r a

0   1500 m
0   1500 yards

① Turkish forces drag 70 light ships across land to complete siege
② Turkish guns bombard defensive walls to create breaches
③ Turkish forces attack weakened walls
④ Turkish forces break through and pillage city

long. When tested, it fired a ball weighing some 1,340 pounds (608 kg) for over a mile before it buried itself in 6 feet (2 meters) of earth.

The Siege Begins

The siege began on April 2, 1453. The sultan's ships crowded around the sea walls of the city to exclude any relief boats. The citizens of Constantinople prevented the sultan's ships from entering the bay to the north of the city, called the Golden Horn, by pulling a massive chain across its entrance. Despite attempts by Turkish galleys to ram the chain, it remained unbroken.

On April 6, a massive bombardment began with the 200 cannons firing about a hundred rounds each and every day. The stone and iron balls crashed into the ancient walls and ground the stone and brick to dust. The defending forces ran from breach to breach, throwing down rubble and working through the night to repair any damage. The military defense was organized by the Emperor Constantine and an Italian nobleman, Giovanni Giustiniani Longo, who was experienced in siege warfare and brought with him his own private army of seven hundred men.

After two weeks, a section of the land wall finally gave in to the relentless cannonade. The stones crumbled and Mehmet ordered a major assault against this section. At night, Turkish warriors scrambled over the rubble and threw themselves at the Greek and Italian soldiers who fought hand-to-hand to force them back. Two hundred Turks were said to have died in the nocturnal assault, but not a single Christian.

Days later, a further clash bolstered the hopes of the defenders. Three Italian galleys and a Byzantine transport ship piled with corn sailed into view of the city. Turkish warships swarmed towards them, expecting to overwhelm with ease the four boats, but the wind was in the favor of the Italians, pushing them toward the city and making it hard for the Turks to maneuver. When the Turks finally caught up with them, it was again the Italians who had the advantage: Their ships were taller than the Turkish galleys, so they could bombard the Turks with arrows and javelins. Mehmet could see the battle from the shore and rode his horse into the water in his excitement.

Seeing his commander watching the conflict, the Turkish admiral personally led his warship against the Italian boats, but his cannonballs fell short and the Italians fought back with showers of arrows. When the Turks attempted to board the enemy ships, the Italians cut at their hands and heads with their swords, dislodging them so that they fell into the sea. Meanwhile, the Byzantine food ship was in great danger of being forced away from the others, so the Italians lashed together all four ships to form one great floating castle. Momentarily stalling in the the straits known as the Bosporous, the defenders on the walls of the city feared that the sailors would eventually be overwhelmed by the sheer numbers of their attackers, but the wind picked up and the floating fortress sailed on toward the Golden Horn, splintering many of the smaller Turkish ships in its path. At night, the defenders lowered the great chain and allowed the four ships into the bay. Although they raised spirits, these little victories did little to solve the problem of diminishing rations and insufficient soldiers to man the walls. Mehmet was growing impatient. Every day of the siege put pressure on his own army as well as the city. Soldiers had to be fed, but the surrounding land was like a desert because the Byzantines had taken the best of the food for themselves. Money was pouring from his war chest yet he had little to show for it. He needed a sign to demonstrate his stranglehold on the city; if nothing was to be delivered to him, he would make it happen himself. He ordered thousands of his men to build a road from the Bosporous to the Golden Horn. Iron wheels were cast and iron rails laid on the road. Next, he ordered 70 of his warships to be lifted ashore and mounted on these wheels. Slowly but surely, being pulled by hundreds of oxen and men, each ship was transported across land and lowered into the city's impregnable bay. The defenders were dumbfounded.

Mehmet could now attack the Greek and Italian ships within the bay and seal off its northern wall. All the sailors captured by his warships were paraded on the shore and executed. In retaliation, the Byzantines marched out their Turkish captives and had their heads cut off. The meaning was clear. Hereon, there would be no quarter given or taken. The citizens of Constantinople would have to fight to the end, and the omens were not good. By the middle of May, food was running low; even fish could not be caught in the Golden Horn as Turkish boats patrolled outside the walls.

On May 28, the Turkish camps outside the walls went remarkably quiet. A few citizens dared to hope it meant that Mehmet was leaving, but the opposite was true. The sultan had ordered his soldiers to prepare for one final great attack. Having gathered all their weapons and replenished their supply of cannonballs and arrows, the troops

Right: *Ottoman cavalry at the siege of Constantinople, wearing different turbans and hats as a mark of status and to denote their unit. Taken from a fresco in the Romanian monastery of Moldovita, painted c.1537.*

Left: *Turkish cannon pound the ancient walls of Constantinople. It was Mehmet's intensive use of artillery during the siege that played a crucial part in undermining the Byzantine defense. From a painting by J.H. Valda.*

were now resting. Early the next morning, a dreadful cacophony rang around the walls of the city. The drums and trumpets of the Turkish army announced the first waves of attack. Hastily recruited troops armed with anything at hand were herded against the great walls. These were the dispensable warriors, preparing the way for the sultan's better troops. They pushed siege towers against the walls and threw up ladders against the piles of rubble, scrambling over the stones to get to the battlements. Giustiniani was in the thick of the defense, wearing armor and hacking at the Turks with his sword. The defenders hurled arrows, rocks, and pots containing "Greek Fire," a concoction of oil and chemicals which created a napalm-like liquid fire.

Despite a ferocious assault, the first wave of Turks was beaten back; but Mehmet had anticipated this. It had served its purpose of draining the defenders' energy. He then sent in a second wave of Turkish soldiers from his homeland. They fought harder and longer, but still the

Byzantines held their battlements, the fear of conquest and death forcing them into greater feats of endurance. Mehmet was beginning to doubt himself, and he flew into a rage. He ordered his final wave of loyal and elite Janissaries to march towards the wall. To the sound of their drums, the Janissaries hurled themslves up the banks of rubble and clashed with the defenders, who by now had been fighting non-stop for five hours. A stray shot from a cannon battered into the chest of Giustiniani and he fell to the ground. Constantine wanted his body left on the battlements, but his men insisted they remove it. As Giustiniani and his followers left the wall, the morale of the other defenders broke under the weight of attack. Janissaries surged over the battlements, prompting many citizens to run from the walls to join their families at home. The great walls had been breached and with them the hopes of the city. Constantine could now see there was little point in organizing further defense; rather than be taken alive, he and his closest companions rushed into

the mass of attacking warriors and were cut down as they fought to the end. It was a worthy end for the very last Roman emperor.

Some citizens managed to scramble into boats in the Golden Horn and escape from the Turkish ships, but the majority fell victim to a day of looting, rape, and massacre in which Mehmet allowed his men to run amok. Before the day ended, Mehmet rode his horse into the city of the Caesars and entered the great church of St. Sophia. Henceforth, it would be a mosque.

Today, the great minarets erected as a result of the sultan's victory stand around the ancient Byzantine dome, built in the sixth century. The remains of the massive walls that Mehmet broke through still stand as a monument to his incredible achievement.

But one thing that does not remain is the name of the city: Constantinople, once the greatest bastion of Christianity, had become the capital of a Muslim empire, and its name lost its Christian connotations, becoming Istanbul.

NAGASHINO 1575

The Japanese general Nobunaga organized his foot soldiers to fire in rotation. The resulting fusillades devastated the charge of the opposing cavalry, and anticipated the disciplined use of firearms in western warfare by many decades.

A Samurai warrior; some were reluctant to adopt the new firearms, preferring their traditional skills of archery.

In Japan, the sixteenth century was a time of relentless civil wars in which everyone fought each other for power—lords against lords, clans against clans. Even the religious orders of Buddhist monks put armies into the field to fight against the Samurai, knights who had perfected their martial art skills. Into this chaotic mix of medieval feuding came a new invention, a weapon that transformed Japanese warfare just as it had transformed warfare across the other side of the world. The new weapon was

the gun and its most devastating demonstration was at the battle of Nagashino in 1575. The gun found its way to Japan from Europe in 1542 when a ship containing Portuguese merchants sailed into a storm in the western Pacific Ocean. The rough seas knocked the ship off course and the Portuguese found themselves stranded on Tanega-shima, an island off the coast of Kyushu, the southernmost part of Japan. As they waded through the surf onto the beach, they were surrounded by the local people. The vision of the sailors dressed in black and carrying strange weapons caused much consternation to the islanders, for the Portuguese were the first Europeans to set foot in Japan.

Explosion like Lightning

A Japanese eyewitness described the new weapon held by the Portuguese: "something two or three feet long, straight on the outside with a passage inside, and made of a heavy substance. At its side there is an aperture which is the passageway for fire. The explosion that it makes is like lightning and the report that it makes is just like thunder."

The weapons brought by the Portuguese were firearms of the type known as the arquebus, a matchlock-operated gun that was lighter than the musket and which therefore did not need a forked rest to support it. The Japanese immediately realised the potential of the Portugese guns, and the local warlord instructed his swordsmiths to copy them. One metalworker is believed to have

swapped his daughter for information on some of the more technical details relating to their manufacture. Within ten years, Japanese-made guns had made their appearance on the battle-field, and one warlord wrote to his followers telling them to "decrease the numbers of spears and have your most capable men carry guns."

As in Europe, however, the appearance of guns was not welcomed by everyone. The martial arts in Japan were highly evolved and many warriors had spent years perfecting their skills in archery and using the spear and sword. The Samurai, like the knights in the West, believed that it was beneath their dignity to use guns, as their reputations as warriors were based on their prowess in hand-to-hand combat. They felt that guns should be used by their social inferiors; the ashigaru. Letting the ashigaru use the guns meant that these lowly soldiers were no longer mere rabble to be ridden over in battle, but a force to be reckoned with. Their consequent elevation in importance also had the effect of raising the status of their Samurai masters. In recognition of this, some of the more farsighted warlords now clad their gun-

The site of Nagashino castle today, on high ground in the center of the picture at the point where the two rivers meet. A naturally strong position difficult to capture by a direct assault.

carrying ashigaru in a simple uniform and began to organize them as a disciplined group. The samurai performed as officers, who directed the ranks of gunmen. One of the most astute of these new warlords was Oda Nobunaga, a man who would begin the process of political unification in Japan. As early as 1549, he had ordered 500 arquebuses for his followers, but he knew it was

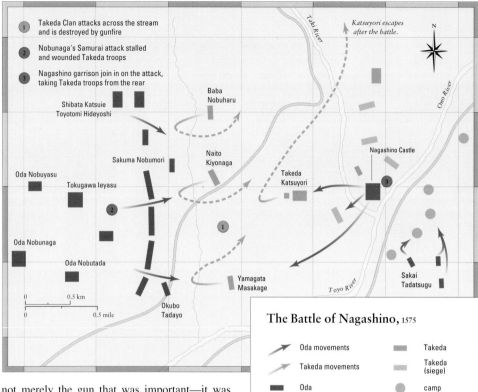

① Takeda Clan attacks across the stream and is destroyed by gunfire

② Nobunaga's Samurai attack stalled and wounded Takeda troops

③ Nagashino garrison join in on the attack, taking Takeda troops from the rear

Katsuyori escapes after the battle.

Taki River

Ono River

N

Baba Nobuharu

Shibata Katsuie
Toyotomi Hideyoshi

Nagashino Castle

Sakuma Nobumori

Naito Kiyonaga

Takeda Katsuyori

Oda Nobuyasu

Tokugawa Ieyasu

Oda Nobunaga

Oda Nobutada

Yamagata Masakage

Toyo River

Sakai Tadatsugu

Okubo Tadayo

0   0.5 km
0   0.5 mile

The Battle of Nagashino, 1575

→ Oda movements
→ Takeda movements
■ Oda

▬ Takeda
▬ Takeda (siege)
● camp

not merely the gun that was important—it was how it was handled and how the men firing the guns were organized. In this process, he was to initiate a revolution in Japanese warfare.

"Stand firm!"

Oda Nobunaga was born in 1534 into a family which had only recently risen in status. His father was a landowner who had spent a decade increasing his control of Owari province in central Japan. At the age of 17, Nobunaga's father died and Nobunaga was thrust into a vicious power struggle, contending as much with his own family as other clans. Over 20 years, Nobunaga perfected the skills of warfare, adding inventive ideas of his own. At the Battle of Okehazama, Nobunaga was hopelessly outnumbered but

created a fake army out of straw stuffed into armor and then led a surprise attack which culminated in lopping the head off the opposition leader. It was an assault worthy of Alexander the Great, and like Alexander's victory at Gaugamela, in 331 B.C., it was a turning point, for

Below : *Reconstructed palisade on the battlefield of Nagashino today. Behind this fence, Nobunaga's arquebusiers volley fired their guns at the cavalry emerging out of the forest.*

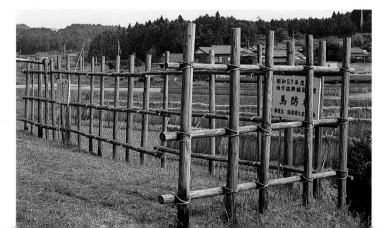

Nobunaga was now one of the leading power-brokers in Japan. He marched on the capital of Kyoto and installed one his own followers as Shogun, but the fighting was far from over. There followed years of campaigns against the warrior monks who contested his power. Nobunaga became a patron of the newly arrived Christians, and Samurai warriors rode into battle shouting "Santa Maria!"

In 1575, an act of defiance occurred at the castle of Nagashino in Mikawa province in central Japan that drew out the full fury of Nobunaga. The castle was built on a naturally high position where two rivers met between cliffs and was held for Nobunaga by a young Samurai called Okudaira Sadamasa. On June 16, the castle was attacked by a force led by Takeda Katsuyori, a leading member of the Takeda clan who had bitterly opposed Nobunaga in previous years. At first, Takeda hoped to take it by a direct assault using boats and siege towers, but Sadamasa defended the castle bravely. Katsuyori decided on a siege. The defenders only had enough food for a few days so Sadamasa sent messengers to Nobunaga, pleading for help. One succeeded in passing through the enemy lines, and Nobunaga replied that he would bring a relieving army to the castle in a few days. The messenger returned with the good news but was intercepted by the Takeda who said they would spare his life if he told the defenders they had no chance of relief and had better surrender immediately. The messenger reluctantly agreed. In order to ensure he passed on this false message, the Takeda tied him to a cross and, surrounded by spearmen, it was raised in front of the castle battlements. The messenger breathed in deeply and shouted out to the defenders: "Within three days you will be rescued. Stand firm!" Immediately, the Takeda soldiers plunged their spears into the brave messenger, but his courage had given the defenders hope.

The Showdown

Nobunaga raised an army of nearly 40,000 warriors and rode to the castle, vowing to crush the Takeda clan once and for all. The Takeda force was barely half this strong, and Katsuyori's retainers advised him to leave, but Katsuyori also wanted a showdown and his smaller force was a highly professional one. At the core of the Takeda army was a fiercesome array of Samurai cavalry clad in armor and bristling with weapons whereas Nobunaga's was merely an amateur force. Nobunaga was aware of the disparity in quality between the two armies and therefore prepared for the combat accordingly. He chose the battlefield well—high ground behind a stream a mile away from the castle. To reinforce this position he used ropes and stakes to make a series of fences or palisades behind which his soldiers could shelter from an attack by horsemen. He then made regular gaps in the palisade to allow for any counterattacks. These fences have since been reconstructed and can be seen on the battlefield of Nagashino today.

Having secured his position, Nubunaga now calculated the most effective way that he could use his army. He had some 3,000 men armed with firearms, but he understood that the guns were slow to load and had only a very short range, making them highly vulnerable to an attack by Samurai cavalry. He could place his army behind the palisade, but he made a further instruction which puts Nobunaga right in the forefront of the history of firearms. He ordered his 3,000-strong ranks of arquebusiers to fire alternating vollies. It was the first major use of this innovative method of rotating firepower anywhere in the world. Many Samurai were ordered to dismount to serve as officers in the firing ranks and to provide

Suicide of Takeda Katsuyori as Nobunaga's warriors finally track him down after the battle of Nagashino had severely reduced his military strength.

armed support for the gunmen. Other Samurai protected the flanks of the arquebusiers. To initiate the battle on the morning of June 29, Nobunaga placed a small force of Samurai in front of the palisade. Katsuyori took the bait. Having organized his army into three great waves of horsemen and footsoldiers, the Takeda warriors rode forward. The previous night it had rained—and, as at Waterloo 250 years later – the clinging mud slowed down the Takeda advance. Katsuyori had hoped the rain would ruin the guns of Nobunaga, but the gunners had kept their fuses dry. Because of the mud, the horsemen were not very swift in their attack and as they swept towards the edge of the stream and the front of palisade, a thousand arquebuses together erupted into fire and a tangle of horses and men in armor collapsed before the stockade. Those left standing urged their horses forward, but a second synchronized volley tore into them, and as they struggled to get to their feet, a third volley cracked like thunder and broke up and decimated the Takeda ranks. An eerie silence was broken by the shrieks of animals and men and then the first rank of Nobunaga's gunmen reloaded and fired again, beginning a second cycle of three volleys. The effect was totally devastating. Nobunaga's Samurai then rushed between the gaps in the palisade and threw themselves onto the wrecked Takeda lines, slashing and stabbing at them with their long spears and swords.

The final blow came when the defenders of Nagashino Castle could see the Takeda clan under heavy attack and rushed out of the castle to hit them in the rear. The defeat was complete. Many of the most noble members of the Takeda clan had been slaughtered in the fire storm, but Katsuyori, whose impetuosity had led to the disaster, escaped to carry on his campaign. His strength, however, was much reduced and he was no longer a serious threat to the man who had almost succeeded in unifying the whole of Japan under his banner.

By the time Nobunaga died in 1582, every Japanese army had at least a third of its soldiers armed with guns, and the rise in the use of firearms and cannon began a period of castle-building in which the advantage now lay with the defender. Not only had Nobunaga transformed his country politically, he had also transformed the style of Japanese warfare.

NASEBY 1645

The use of hills to prevent the enemy from gaining an accurate idea of Parliamentarian forces was a key to their success against the king. The monarch paid for the failure of his scouts with his life, and England became a short-lived republic.

Oliver Cromwell (1599–1658), who commanded the Parliamentarian cavalry at Naseby, from a painting attributed to Van Dyck. Cromwell established the highly disciplined Ironsides, drawn initially from his native eastern counties where his family held modest estates. After his key role in securing victory for Parliament in the war, Cromwell went on to become a reluctant Protector in which he had extensive powers.

Naseby was the decisive battle of the English Civil War, the culmination of three years of conflict between Roundheads and Cavaliers. As a result of this one battle, a king lost his kingdom and—in due course—his life, and England became (albeit temporarily) a republic.

King and Parliament

The English Civil War, like so many conflicts across western Europe in the seventeenth century, began as a challenge to established authority. A Catholic monarchy was no longer acceptable to a largely Protestant middle class, and relations between King Charles I and Parliament broke down into armed conflict. The king could call upon enormous financial resources and the experience of professional commanders, but slowly and effectively Parliament forged its own well-trained forces in the form of the New Model Army led by Thomas Fairfax and Oliver Cromwell. It was these two forces that clashed on the morning of June 14, 1645 about a mile (1.6 km) northwest of the Northamptonshire village of Naseby, in the heart of England.

A Hidden Army

Earlier in the summer, Fairfax had led his New Model Army toward the city of Oxford, the very heart of the king's support. Charles wanted to lure him away from there, and Fairfax—hungry for confrontation—followed him out of the city. Both were poised for conflict, and were impatient for a decisive battle.

Charles was uncertain of the numbers opposing him and pondered his predicament. The rolling hills around Naseby served to hide his forces, but similarly they prevented a true calculation of the enemy. He sent out scouts but they reported seeing very few of the rebels. Prince Rupert, one of the king's professional commanders, set out to assess for himself the enemy strength. He saw Parliamentarian cavalry retreating before his own small force. Prince Rupert was a dashing character—a classic cavalier, full of courage and action—and in his view this was the sign of a discouraged foe who needed just a hard blow to send them packing. In reality, the horsemen he saw were Parliamentarian scouts; the surrounding hills hid a 13,000-strong Parliamentarian army—outnumbering his own troops by 4,000. Rupert returned to his king and recommended a fight.

Charles rapidly galvanized his army into action. A core of 4,000 footsoldiers was flanked by some 5,000 cavalry. Typical of the day and common to both sides, the footsoldiers were made up of units of men armed with muskets. These soldiers were shielded by further units which were armed with long pikes to protect them from cavalry. Fairfax arranged his soldiers in a similar manner, with cavalry on the flanks. He also concealed a regiment known as

Charles I (1600–49), King of England and overall commander of the Royalist forces at Naseby. During his captivity in the wake of Naseby, Charles continued to plot against Parliament, leading to his 'trial' at Westminster and bravely faced execution.

Right: *Charles I's battle plans drawn up prior to the battle of Naseby. His army is shown at the top of the picture, ready to advance toward Mill Hill. The typical arrangement of units of pikemen alternating with musketeers is clearly shown, as are the units of cavalry on the flanks.*

Okey's Dragoons behind a hedge along the left wing. The objective in this kind of warfare was to turn the opponent's flank and thus roll up the center, surrounding the enemy and throwing him into confusion. Prince Rupert was well experienced in these tactics and was aware that the advantage lay with a swift and overwhelming attack. In the rush to strike, the Royalist forces found themselves advancing up a slope toward the enemy. As Fairfax brought his men over the ridge, the full enormity of the Parliamentarian force was revealed. The Royalists must at that point have wondered at the wisdom of the assault. It would certainly seem that Prince Rupert was spurred into a "do-or-die" frame of mind. Taking command of the cavalry on his right flank, he swung his sword high in the air, leading almost 2,000 Royalist cavalry in a thundering charge.

Dashing Cavalry

Earlier in the Civil War, the reckless charges of the Royalist cavalry had been something to fear, but now the Parliamentarians were prepared for such an attack. Fairfax had scattered the field with his dragoons, who used horses for mobility but fought on foot with muskets. Acting in a similar role to the Special Forces of today, the dragoons would snipe at the enemy, using the cover of a hedge to attack the Royalist horsemen and knock many from their saddles. The impetus of the Royalist charge was not helped by the uphill slope. By the time they surged into the Parliamentarian lines of cavalry, they encountered an enemy

who was trained to stand and fight. Firing pistols before contact, and then laying into the enemy with swords, the two sides fought ferociously, each seeking to gain the upper hand.

In the center of the battle, meanwhile, the Royalist footsoldiers had joined the general advance and were pushing hard on the Parliamentarian foot. Feeling they had done well enough to survive the Royalist cavalry onslaught, some of the Parliamentarian cavalry now moved across to assist their own footsoldiers against the Royalist center, but Prince Rupert was not one to give up so easily. It was here that his personal courage helped to create the opportunity that caused the first great crisis of the battle.

Rupert rallied his cavalry, called in his reserves, and led a second charge against the Parliamentarian cavalry. "Charging with incredible valor and fury," wrote a contemporary, Rupert "broke in upon and routed the three rightmost Divisions of that Left Wing." The Parliamentarian cavalry disintegrated, and at this point the battle could have been won.

With the Parliamentarian center under pressure and its left flank in tatters, Rupert could have turned the full force of his horsemen on the center and rolled up the Parliamentarian army. At this vital point, however, the unfettered instincts of victorious men on horseback took over. Rather than exert control and tactical discipline, the Royalist cavalry charged straight through the remnants of the enemy and right off the battlefield to loot the Parliamentarian baggage train over a mile (1.6 km) away. By the time they returned to the battlefield, events had swung against the king's forces and the Parliamentarians were on the offensive.

While Rupert and his men indulged in their looting spree, the Parliamentarian footsoldiers were taking a severe hammering. Left almost isolated by the retreat of their comrades, Skippon's Regiment stood and fought Lord Astley's Royalist infantry, muskets firing point blank at each other, their commanders falling wounded. Up against Charles's veteran soldiers of the Oxford Army, anyone else would have broken and fled, but this was the "preaching

The battlefield today, looking north from the lines held by the Parliamentarians along Sibbertoft Road. Cromwell's Ironsides would have pursued the retreating Royalists across this ground.

and praying regiment" of hardened Protestants. Their ferocious struggle was a test of faith. Two hundred years later, a mass grave was discovered on the spot where Skippon's Regiment stood and suffered the greatest casualties of the Parliamentarian army. This localized action was the real crisis point of the battle for the Parliamentarians. By standing solid, Skippon's Regiment gave time for Fairfax to bring in his reserves and for Okey's Dragoons to join the attack on Astley. The focus of the battle now

Typical pikeman of the English Civil War, from an engraving published in 1786. Many pikemen discarded their armor in order to gain flexibility.

An Officer of Pikemen.

shifted to the right flank where Oliver Cromwell commanded his elite Ironside cavalry.

Piling on the Pressure

Advancing at a controlled pace and with pistols raised, Cromwell's Ironsides swept aside the Royalist cavalry opposite them and turned in on the Royalist footsoldiers in the center. The Royalists put up a terrific defense: pikes thrusting, muskets blazing, they were the finest of Charles's followers and would not let down their king easily. Fairfax piled on the pressure. His center advanced, his dragoons and remaining cavalry on the left wing closed in, and Cromwell's Ironsides were relentless. In danger of being surrounded, the Royalist army gave way, but it was a fighting retreat. (Musket balls discovered under the battlefield in recent years show that the Royalist army must have been pushed back over two miles [3.2 km].) A desperate King Charles, seeing the best of his men being slaughtered, had to be held back by his supporters from personally leading a countercharge. It was too late for such acts of heroism.

When Prince Rupert eventually returned to the battlefield over an hour after his victorious charge, all he saw was destruction. A group of Royalist footsoldiers was surrounded and within minutes, these loyal men were either killed or captured. (A concentration of musket balls found here reveals the storm of fire they must have endured.) Rupert rode on to join the remnants of his broken army scattering to the north. A final attempt at rallying his troops was attempted, but Fairfax was relentless and brought his men together to attack in an orderly formation. With dragoons sniping at them and the Parliamentarians pouring pistol and musket fire into their weakened and retreating ranks, the Royalists had had enough. They were routed.

Fairfax ordered his cavalry not to loot the

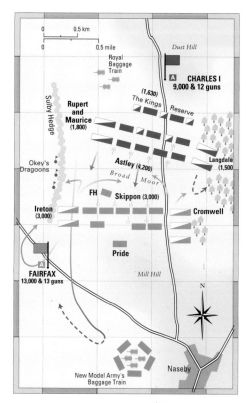

Battle of Naseby, June 14, 1645

▮ Infantry unit		❚❙❙ Artillery	
◥ Cavalry unit		→ Royalist advance	
♪ small cavalry unit		→ Parliamentarian advance	

enemy baggage train but to hunt down fleeing soldiers. He wanted it to be a decisive battle, without the risk of the king's forces reuniting. That afternoon and evening, Cromwell's Ironsides pursued the remnants of the enemy.

The defeat of the Royalists was complete. Over 5,000 soldiers were taken prisoner and the Royalist artillery fell into Parliamentary hands as did Charles's private correspondence. Although the king's power was broken, it was a year before the Civil War ended.

WATERLOO 1815

*Wellington knew the value of preparation. He knew the
land south of Brussels and chose his ground well. His army
of British, German, Dutch, and Belgian troops would make
its stand against the French around two farmhouses.*

*The Duke of Wellington
(1769–1852), as painted by
Francisco Goya in 1812.
(Although Goya managed to
retain his position as court
portrait painter under Joseph
Bonaparte during the French
occupation of Spain, it is his
images of barbarous cruelty
during the conflict that are his
best known works of this
period.) It was in Spain that
Wellington had a series
of victories in the drive to
expel the French from the
Iberian peninsula. He
displayed the exceptional
understanding of sound
logistics that he had
developed in Indian
campaigns.*

The Duke of Wellington had the measure of the French. For six years he had fought them as commander of British forces in the Peninsular War, chasing them through Portugal, Spain, and eventually across the Pyrenees back into France. He had learned to counter their aggressive tactics, instructing his men to lie down to avoid their barrage of cannon fire, and ordering his own gunners to load grape-shot to shatter their cavalry charges and dense columns of infantry. But he had never fought against Napoleon, the most brilliant commander of his age.

Rain and Mud

It was at the battle of Waterloo that these two military giants finally met—and the outcome determined the fate of Europe for a hundred years. In 1814, many considered the war between France and the rest of Europe to be over. Napoleon had been forced into exile at Elba and a treaty concluding hostilities was signed, but the emperor could not relinquish his dream of European conquest and escaped from his island confinement. He sailed back to France where his old soldiers returned to his side and the newly restored French monarchy fled before him.

In Vienna, four great nations—Austria, Great Britain, Prussia, and Russia—raised a million men to oppose him. Napoleon knew he must move quickly to defeat them army by army and

struck into Belgium where the British and Prussian armies had formed. The latter was defeated by Napoleon's mastery of tactics at Ligny earlier in 1815. Napoleon then sent his troops after the British, forcing them to fight a desperate rearguard action at Quatre-Bras. It looked as though the emperor's strategic genius had worked once more, but Wellington, based in Brussels, was biding his time.

Wellington was well aware of the value of preparation. He knew the land south of Brussels and chose his ground well. His army, composed of British, German, Dutch, and Belgian troops, would make its stand in the fields outside the village of Waterloo. With his years of experience, Wellington also knew exactly the kind of battle he would have to fight: a defensive one. He realized this for two reasons. Firstly, he had been assured by the Prussian commander Gebhard von Blücher that if he could but hold the French, the Prussians would come to his aid. Secondly, he saw that this would be an effective way of absorbing the aggressive French tactics. On the eve of battle, however, a third reason presented itself. Great sheets of rain poured down as Wellington's men marched to their positions at Waterloo. The fields turned into quagmires of thick, sucking mud that had soldiers stumbling, slowed horses, and trapped artillery.

On the morning of June 18, the rain finally stopped and the sun broke through, but there was no dawn attack. The mud bogged down

*Napoleon Bonaparte
(1769–1821), painted by Paul
Delaroche, famed for his
historical portraits. Born in
Corsica, Napoleon developed
military skills that helped him
rise to the rank of general
during the French
Revolutionary Wars. It was in
1799 on his return from a
failed campaign in Egypt,
intended to harm Britain's
trade, that he seized power
and became the autocrat of
France.*

The farmhouse at Hougoumont today, whose thick walls provided a makeshift fort for Wellington's elite Foot Guards.

Farmhouse

Garden wall

Grenadier guards

Coldstream guards

THE MORNING BEFORE THE BATTLE

Many soldiers wrote accounts of their experiences in the war against Napoleon. One of the most vivid is provided by an anonymous soldier of the 71st Highland Regiment. He described the hours before the great battle of Waterloo:

"During the whole night the rain never ceased. Two hours after daybreak General Hill came down... Shortly afterwards we got half an allowance of liquor, which was the most welcome thing I ever received. I was so stiff and sore from the rain I could not move with freedom for some time. A little afterwards, the weather clearing up, we began to clean our arms and prepare for action. The whole of the opposite heights were covered by the enemy.

"A young lad who had joined but a short time before said to me, while we were cleaning: 'Tom, you are an old soldier, and have escaped often, and have every chance to escape this time also. I am sure I am to fall.' 'Nonsense, be not gloomy.' 'I am certain,' he said. 'All I ask is that you will tell my parents when you get home that I ask God's pardon for the evil I have done and the grief I have given them. Be sure to tell I died praying for their blessing and pardon.' I grew dull myself, but gave him all the heart I could. He only shook his head. I could say nothing to alter his belief."

Later that day, the young man was killed by a cannon ball.

European Grenadier Guards c.1815. Far left, an Old Guard Grenadier of the Imperial Guard which formed the most experienced troops available to Napoleon for the 1814–15 campaign.

everything and everyone; obviously Napoleon would not send his men across such a natural barrier but would wait for the ground to harden. As he waited Wellington took control of the terrain. The majority of Wellington's troops were positioned on the reverse slope of a long ridge running the length of the battlefield. Not only did this protect them from artillery fire, but it also screened them from the vision of the attacking French, allowing them to appear suddenly at the closest range (a tactic Wellington had mastered in Spain). Wellington strengthened his position by sending some of his men to occupy the sturdy farmhouses at La Haye-Sainte and Hougoumont; the contingents based there not only protected his flanks but could also break up any general French advance. Finally, understanding the mixed spirits of his multinational force, Wellington placed his loyal British and German soldiers in the front ranks and his Dutch and Belgians in reserve.

"Vive l'empereur"

Napoleon eventually began the battle around 11 A.M. Like a chess player sizing up his opponent, he could see exactly why Wellington had placed his men in the farmhouse at Hougoumont. So Napoleon planned this to be his first object of attack; by so doing he expected Wellington to draw forward his reserves to reinforce it. This would weaken the British center and allow his main central advance to break through. The farmhouse, however, was an extraordinarily strong building, with its thick walls and slits cut into the bricks allowing troops to fire out. Inside this makeshift fort stood Wellington's Foot Guards, one of his elite units, and they held on to it with iron tenacity during a whole day of fighting. Rather than sucking in British rein-

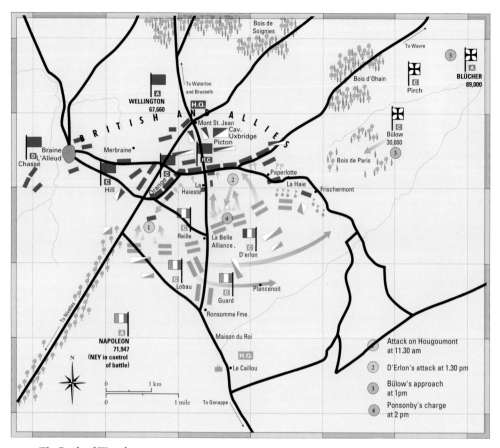

The Battle of Waterloo, June 18 , 1815: the early phases 11 a.m. to 3 p.m.

French commander	**A** army	Allied battalion	infantry unit	Allied position c.4 p.m.
Prussian commander	**C** corps	French battalion	cavalry unit	Allied position c.7 p.m.
Allied commander	**R.C** reserve corps	cavalry picquets	French position c.4 p.m.	Allied direction of movement
	D division	artillery	French position c.7 p.m.	French direction of movement

forcements to support it, the humble stronghold dragged in more and more French troops in the emperor's determination to take it.

As the battle for Hougoumont dragged on, Napoleon ordered a barrage of at least 80 cannons to blast away at the British center.

Cannonballs hissed through the air, bouncing and rolling on the ground to cause hideous injuries to anyone in their path, removing legs, arms, and heads. This was the form of assault soldiers feared most; all they could do was wait in their positions as their comrades were

knocked down one by one. Napoleon depended on this tactic to weaken his enemy, but Wellington had protected the majority of his troops behind the ridge. Consequently, although the cannonade was destructive, its effects were less than devastating. After almost an hour of this, Napoleon sent in his columns of troops. Shouting "Vive l'empereur!" and marching proudly and confidently to the sound of their drums, the French formations must have been a formidable sight.

Immediately, two British forward positions were overrun and the French columns rolled up the slope to the ridge. A Dutch-Belgian brigade, having had their nerves pushed to breaking point by the cannonade, took one look at the advancing French, turned, and ran. But the British veterans had seen it all before. They just stood, trusted their commander, and when the time came, advanced over the ridge and fired their muskets at close range. With bayonets fixed, they bellowed a blood curdling cheer and charged the French. It was now the turn of the French to lose their nerve. With the addition of two brigades of British cavalry let off the leash, the French broke and ran back down the slope.

Hand-to-hand Fighting

The fighting became fierce and hand-to-hand, swords cutting and slashing. Sergeant Charles Ewart of the Greys, possibly the most famous hero of the day, seized the opportunity to grab at the eagle standard of a French Regiment, but it would not come easily. His vivid account of the struggle evokes the brutal nature of the battlefield. "It was in the charge I took the Eagle from the enemy," he recalled. "He and I had a hard contest for it; he made a thrust at my groin, I parried it off and cut him down through the head. After this a Lancer came at me; I threw the lance down by my right side, and cut him through the chin and upwards through the teeth. Next a footsoldier fired at me, and then charged me with his bayonet, which I also had the good luck to parry and then I cut him down through the head; thus ended the contest."

Cavalry Attack

Napoleon had failed to break the British center and now there was a second threat. Blucher's promised Prussian army was advancing toward the battlefield, forcing Napoleon to use his reserve troops to create a second front protecting his right flank. The crisis of the battle had been reached. Napoleon delegated decisions on the British sector to his battlefield commander, Marshal Michel Ney. Believing that one more assault would break British resolve, Ney launched a massive cavalry attack. The French cavalry were among the most skilful of their day and comprised a colorful array of Lancers, Hussars, and armored Cuirassiers. Troop after troop of French cavalry surged up the slope to Wellington's lines, but the British quickly formed themselves into square formations, thus presenting walls of muskets and bayonets to the cavalry as they circled around them.

The squares did not stop the soldiers feeling afraid. "A considerable number of the French cuirassiers made their appearance," recalled a sergeant of the 71st Highland Regiment. "Their appearance, as an enemy, was certainly enough to inspire a feeling of dread—none of them under six feet; defended by steel helmets and breastplates... I thought we could not have the slightest chance with them." But the British kept their nerve and poured volleys of musket-fire into the cavalry, creating a sound like hail on a roof as the balls hit the horsemen's armor. When confronted with a steadfast infantry

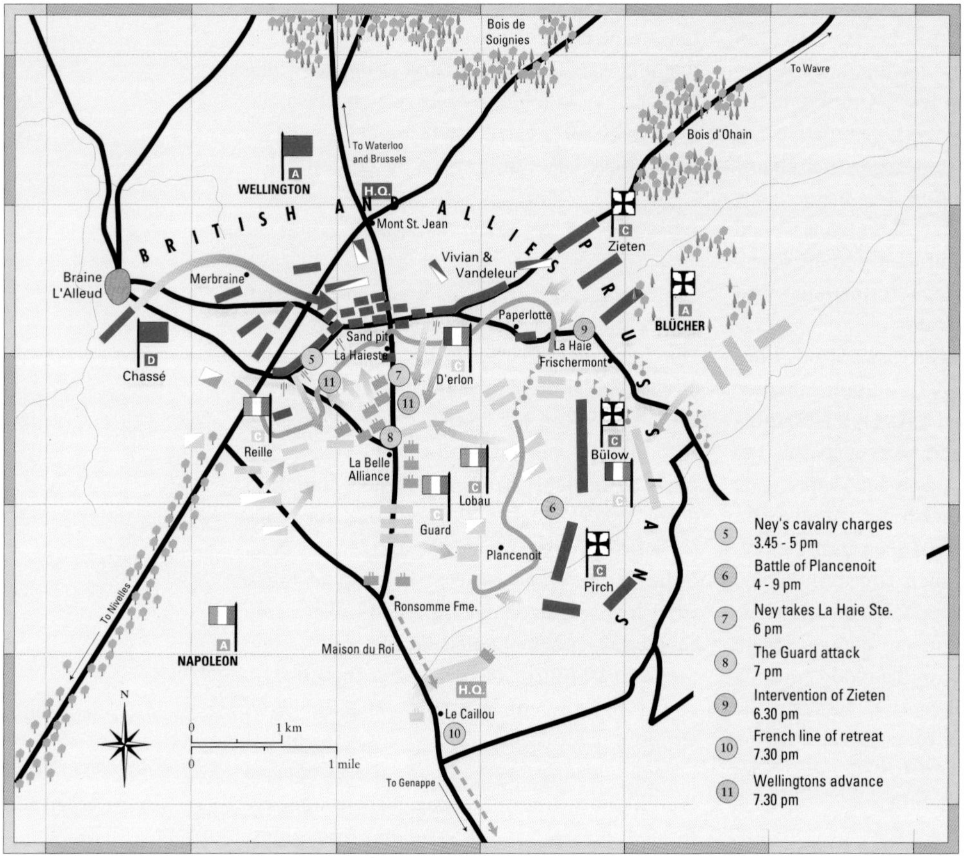
Bois de Soignies
To Wavre
Bois d'Ohain
To Waterloo and Brussels
WELLINGTON
H.Q.
Mont St. Jean
BRITISH AND ALLIES
PRUSSIANS
Zieten
Vivian & Vandeleur
BLÜCHER
Braine L'Alleud
Merbraine
Papelotte
Sand pit
La Haie Ste.
La Haie Frischermont
Chassé
D'erlon
Reille
Bülow
La Belle Alliance
Lobau
Guard
Plancenoit
Pirch
Ronsomme Fme.
To Nivelles
NAPOLEON
Maison du Roi
H.Q.
Le Caillou
0 1 km
0 1 mile
To Genappe
N
Ney's cavalry charges 3.45 - 5 pm
Battle of Plancenoit 4 - 9 pm
Ney takes La Haie Ste. 6 pm
The Guard attack 7 pm
Intervention of Zieten 6.30 pm
French line of retreat 7.30 pm
Wellingtons advance 7.30 pm

The Battle of Waterloo, June 18, 1815: the later phases, 3 p.m. to 7.30 p.m.

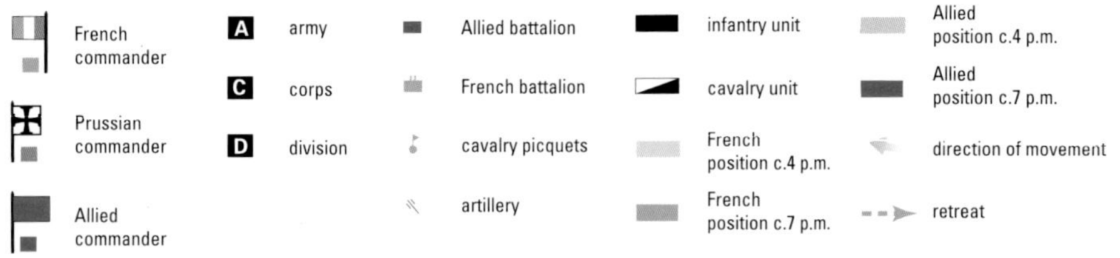
French commander
Prussian commander
Allied commander
army
corps
division
Allied battalion
French battalion
cavalry picquets
artillery
infantry unit
cavalry unit
French position c.4 p.m.
French position c.7 p.m.
Allied position c.4 p.m.
Allied position c.7 p.m.
direction of movement
retreat

formation there is very little that men on horseback can do. Many of the French cavalry were reduced to trotting around the squares, vainly waving their swords and pistols. Ney was forced to withdraw his horsemen when the British cavalry launched a counterattack. But just as the situation for Napoleon was looking desperate, a key element in the British defense broke down.

In the farmhouse of La Haye-Sainte, the German riflemen had run out of ammunition, forcing them to flee. The farmhouse was left to the French who were now in a position to threaten Wellington's left flank. Ney sent in lines of infantry and demanded Napoleon's reserves, but these had already gone to defend their own flank against the approaching Prussians. As his own lines wavered under the French assault, Wellington poured in his reserves. By early evening the lines of red-coated soldiers had recovered their command of the battlefield. The British had managed to remain undefeated.

The Prussians now pushed into the French right flank, threatening to encircle Napoleon's army. It was time for Napoleon's final stroke: he ordered the Old Guard to advance. The Old Guard were his elite soldiers, veterans who had followed him loyally across Europe in victory and defeat. They were the most reliable and courageous of his troops, and their advance had generally been a prelude to victory. In steady step, they marched up the hill past the flaming ruin of Hougoumont—still in British hands. Up the slope they marched until the British stood up on the crest, their previously obscured lines waiting for the French columns. It was the final showdown.

Musket fire erupted in clouds of dense, rolling smoke. Musket balls ripped into the blue-clad columns. The front line troops of the Old Guard staggered. Again and again, the British fired coordinated volleys which shook the French columns. At the end of a long, dangerous day, it was too much to bear, and Napoleon's most faithful troops, his last chance, disintegrated before the British fire. Wellington ordered a general advance and his

Right: *In "Quatre Bras", a painting by Lady Butler, a square of the 28th Foot resists a French cavalry attack.*

troops roared their approval, having finally turned Napoleon back. With Prussians still savaging his flank, Napoleon could see the battle was lost. The retreat turned into a rout as British cavalry surged over the ridge to pursue the French down the slope and off the battlefield. Wellington and the British had won a great historic victory.

The battle of Waterloo was Napoleon's last gasp. The French were exhausted after more than two decades of war, and Napoleon was forced to surrender to the British, who sent him into exile as a prisoner on the island of St. Helena in the south Atlantic. There he remained, still plotting, until he died six years later. Britain and Prussia were now the dominant nations in Europe, and Europe itself would be free of a continent-wide war for a hundred years. With Napoleon defeated, Britain could now focus on enlarging what became the greatest Empire the world has known. Waterloo was treated as a special experience in the lives of every soldier who fought there, each one receiving a medal struck to mark the event. Wellington eventually became Prime Minister.

In contrast, the dead of Waterloo were treated unceremoniously and tipped into a common, unmarked grave. Only later in the century would memorials be erected to the courage of those who died—culminating in a giant mound surmounted by a stone lion which today is the most prominent sight on the battlefield. From the top of this mound, visitors can look across the fields to see the preserved buildings of Hougoumont and La Haye-Sainte which played such a key part in Wellington's defense. A circular building contains a vast painting of the battle. In the nearby village of Waterloo, the house used by Wellington as his headquarters is now a museum, a commemoration of a defining moment in Europe's history.

Alamo 1836

The impossible odds stacked against the heroic defenders of the Alamo, coupled with the colorful exploits of Davy Crockett, have given the battle around the Texan mission post almost legendary status.

David Crockett (1786–1836) was a backwoodsman who made a name for himself fighting the Creek Indians under Andrew Jackson in 1814. In 1821 he was elected to the Tennessee state legislature and five years later to Congress.

In 1836, the state of Texas belonged to Mexico. This land had been conquered by the Spanish conquistadors in the sixteenth century. Following them came Catholic missionaries who defended themselves against the natives by building fortified mission posts. In San Antonio, the capital of Texas, there stood a particularly handsome mission post with a fine stone gateway. It was called the Alamo and would become the scene of one of the most famous last stands in American history.

A Blow for Freedom

Mexico had won its freedom from Spain in 1821. It was now the turn of Anglo-American colonists in Texas to demand freedom from Mexico, and in 1835 they began a rebellion in the state capital. For some years, the Alamo mission post had ceased to be a religious center and was used as a garrison by the Mexican army. In the streets outside the fort, the American rebels forced the Mexican soldiers to retreat and captured the Alamo. They now had a center of resistance. Antonio de Santa Anna, President of Mexico and commander of its army, was furious at this humiliating defeat and immediately led an army to crush the Texan rebellion.

On February 23, 1836, Santa Anna entered San Antonio with an army of 5,000 soldiers. Awaiting them within the Alamo were some 200 Texan patriots, including men, women, and children. Some of them were native Texans rallying to the call for independence, while others were volunteers from the United States coming to help their comrades. Among these defenders were some legendary figures. Davy Crockett was a frontiersman born in Tennessee, famous for his hunting prowess, portrayed in contemporary paintings in buckskins with a racoon hat. He was also a successful politician, and had served three terms in Congress. When he lost his campaign for a fourth term, he raised a dozen Tennessee volunteers and rode south to join the Texans. James Bowie was an adventurer who married well and ended up a wealthy Texan landowner. He was a fierce knife fighter and his name has become associated with the large curved knife he used, although it is not clear whether he or his brother actually invented it. With his wife and children dead following a cholera epidemic, he joined the Texan rebels and held joint command of the forces in the Alamo with Colonel William Travis.

The Texans had done their best to strengthen the mission fort. Earthworks and a stockade were raised outside the walls. Inside, the chapel held a gunpowder magazine, and parapets had been raised behind the walls on which cannons were mounted, but still the defenders were vastly outnumbered. Colonel Travis had sent out a plea for reinforcements, but the only answer he got was a further 32 men and boys from Gonzales who made their way through the Mexican lines to stand beside him. A group of Mexican cavalry approached the fort with a white flag, seeking a quick end to Texan resistance. Two of the Texans went to confer with the Mexicans and returned with Santa Anna's terms. It was unconditional surrender or death. Colonel Travis ordered his reply—a single cannon shot from the walls of the Alamo. The fight had begun.

The Mexicans encircled the Alamo with trenches and gun emplacements and began a continuous bombardment of the mission. They tried to take it by storm during the day and at night, but both times the Texans sent them packing, their sharpshooting frontiersmen proving especially effective. The Mexicans now settled down for a siege, relying on their cannons to wear down the defenders. The Texans responded by leading several raids from the mission, capturing food and burning the Mexican lines. On March 3, the Mexicans cut the water supply to the Alamo by blocking the aqueduct. For ten days, the Texans had held out against a mighty Mexican army, with few casualties of their own, but now it seemed there was to be no relieving force, and Santa Anna was impatient to finish off the siege. Colonel Travis assembled all his defenders and drew a line in the sand with the point of his sword. "Those prepared to give their lives in freedom's cause," he declared, "come over to me."

Plan of the Alamo in 1836, showing the full extent of the fortified mission post with its sturdy walls and outhouses.

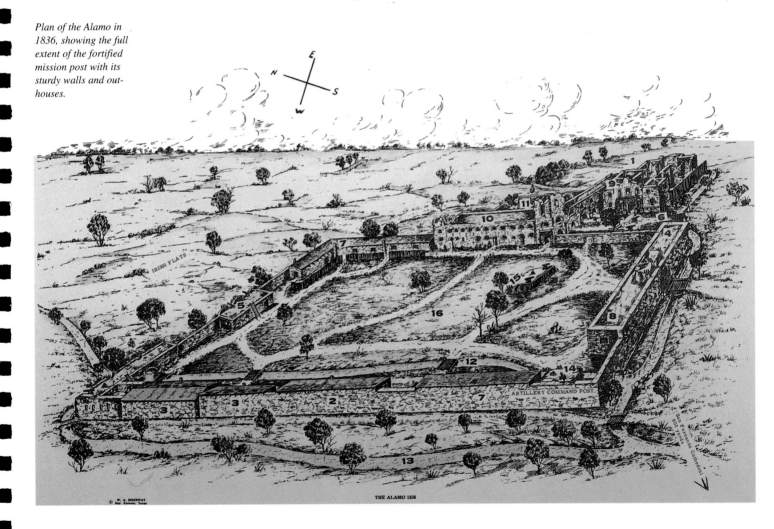

THE ALAMO 1836

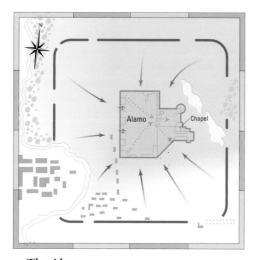

The Alamo, MARCH 6, 1836

— Mexican siege line

↗ Final Mexican assault on the Alamo's walls

⇢ Texan withdrawal to the chapel where the last stand is made

Every one of the defenders, except for one, stepped over the line to stand beside him. Even James Bowie—who was suffering from typhoid and confined to a bed—asked that his cot be carried over the line.

On the morning of March 6, before the sun had risen, an eerie sound was heard by the defenders of the Alamo. Mexican buglers were sounding the "Deguello," a command of no quarter to the Texans. They quickly roused themselves and rushed to the parapets behind the mission walls. In the darkness, they could see columns of Mexicans soldiers advancing to the walls carrying scaling ladders. With muskets, rifles, and pistols, the Texans poured fire into the Mexicans, throwing them off their ladders and forcing them back to their lines. The Mexicans rallied and advanced, and the Texans fired again, forcing them away; but their ammunition was running

Fall of the Alamo, a painting showing the moment when the defenders are overwhelmed by the Mexican army with Davy Crockett swinging his rifle as a club.

short and Santa Anna persisted in his attempt on the walls. A third assault began; this time the ladders stayed against the walls and the Mexican soldiers surged over the parapet. Mrs. Dickinson, wife of one of the defenders, recalled the bitter hand-to-hand fighting: "Unable, from the crowd and want of time, to load their guns and rifles, the Texans made use of the butt ends of the latter, and continued the fight till life ebbed out of their wounds."

Colonel Travis stood on the parapet behind the walls, cheering his men on until a bullet hit him in the face and he slumped across a cannon. The Mexicans swarmed past him into the mission, dragging their cannons into the building to blast away at the heavy doors of the church behind which the defenders now crowded. Davy Crockett, swinging his gun as a club, was shot down inside the chapel and bayonetted. James Bowie, still in his bed, raised himself to fire his pistols as the Mexicans burst into his room and then died under their blows. Only Mrs. Dickinson and 14 other non-combatants were spared the slaughter. The final storming of the mission had lasted less than hour, but the entire siege had cost the Mexican army nearly 1,600 dead soldiers against the slaughter of 182 Texans.

Remember the Alamo

Santa Anna called the storming of the Alamo "a small affair" and had the bodies of its defenders immediately burned. But the repercussions of this combat had only just began. It was a gallant and brave defense of Texan freedom. Within two months, a second army of Texan rebels rode against Santa Anna. This time, just 800 Texans swept away a Mexican army twice as strong at the battle of San Jacinto. Their battle cry was "Remember the Alamo!" Santa Anna was captured, and with this victory Texas gained its independence. In 1845, Texas officially became part of the United States.

Today, all that remains of the Alamo is the chapel with its famous facade. At one stage, it was going to be turned into a hotel, but in 1905, it was bought by the Daughters of the Republic of Texas and turned into a museum and shrine to the memory of its defenders. Since then the symbolism of the Alamo has grown in the minds of all Americans as a sign of their continued desire for freedom from tyranny.

The main gateway to the Alamo Mission, barricaded and defended to the last by the Texans, and known as "the cradle of Texas liberty." The Mission of San Antonio de Valera was founded in 1718 by the Franciscans. The chapel-fort was bought by the State in 1883, and the surrounding area was added in 1905. A three-year restoration program began in 1936.

ANTIETAM 1862

A sunken road proved ideal for the main Confederate defensive position. The repeated assaults by the Northern forces on the well-protected Confederates produced a terrible carnage, which gave the battle its awful reputation.

Abraham Lincoln (in top hat) on the battlefield of Antietam. Opposite him stands General McClellan, commander of the Union army.

Antietam was renowned as the bloodiest single day of the American Civil War; it was as though the colorful regiments of the age of Napoleon were lined up in the killing fields of the First World War. During the second half of the nineteenth century, technical developments altered the balance of strength and tactics on the battlefield. Warfare no longer favored the sweeping assault over the static, unimaginative defender: Improved guns, repeating rifles, and more accurate artillery created a devastating arc of fire that shifted the balance of power toward the entrenched, well-defended army. Some commanders took time to recognize this change.

The Lost Order

Despite the strategic odds stacked against the Confederate army, it confounded everyone's predictions by beginning the Civil War with victories against the industrialized North. In the second year of the war, 1862, the most daring and revered of Confederate generals, Robert E. Lee, decided to prosecute the war against the North with an offensive campaign. Lee was a Napoleonic general who believed in maneuver warfare with mobile columns of troops constantly wrong-footing the enemy. With his 55,000-strong army of Northern Virginia, he invaded Northern territory, threateningly close to Washington. Opposing him was George B. McClellan with his army of the Potomac, approximately 97,000 strong.

Despite being outnumbered almost two to one, Lee split his army by sending one of his ablest commanders, Stonewall Jackson, to capture Harper's Ferry 17 miles (27 km) to the south. This took longer than expected, developing into a siege, and Lee then found his troops spread out and divided by the Potomac River. McClellan was a cautious commander—perhaps understandably considering the initial Northern defeats—but even he should have seen the virtue of destroying Lee's army piece by piece. His luck was further enhanced when the Confederate battle orders were lost and then found by his own troops, giving him details of Confederate plans and dispositions. At this point, the time was ripe for a swift, overwhelming attack, but McClellan took his time, allowing Lee to concentrate his forces near the town of Sharpsburg. At the last moment, Jackson succeeded in capturing Harper's Ferry and rushed to reinforce Lee, although even then the Confederates had only 45,000 men to McClellan's 90,000.

Valuable days were allowed to slip by as McClellan pondered what to do next. The Confederates were effectively trapped around the small town of Sharpsburg with the unfordable Potomac River behind them. If McClellan got it right, this could be the decisive and crushing defeat of the Confederate army he was looking for, with little room to escape to fight again. But as McClellan waited, gathering his large force around him, Lee was busy preparing the battleground. He could only fight a defensive battle and he made sure the ground was secure in front of his positions. Antietam Creek provided a useful barrier screening his right flank, restricting the Northern Army to attack over the bridges or through the creek. On his center-left flank, Lee took command of a sunken road which formed an improvised line of trenches. Only his far left flank was vulnerable.

On the morning of September 17, McClellan finally felt confident enough to launch his massive attack on the small Confederate forces. In the half-light of dawn, line upon line of blue-coated soldiers advanced against the weakest point of Lee's defense—his left flank. They stumbled

The fierce fighting at Burnside's Bridge with the Union army on the left advancing into Confederate fire, as depicted in a lithograph by Kurz and Allison.

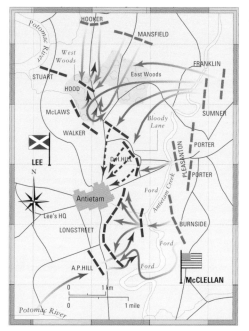

through the cornfield into a withering hail of rebel fire and took a terrible toll. Muskets and rifles cracked in the early morning gloom. Positioned in a small wood behind Dunker Church, the Confederates stood their ground, trading shot for shot with the superior Northern forces. The Confederates, cheered by their ability to stop the Northern advance, gradually pushed them out of the wood, forcing the Northern lines back to Miller Farm.

But the battle was not to be won so easily. Northern forces counterattacked through another wood and pushed the Confederates back to the church. Since it was a stalemate situation, Lee decided to use his reserve forces in a final attempt to hold his left flank. If this didn't work, his whole army could be rolled up behind their defensive positions. It was a gamble, but it is also a sign of good generalship, to know when to commit valuable troops. Lee sent them into the fighting around the church, and they caught the Northern troops in a devastating crossfire. The left flank was saved, forcing McClellan to look elsewhere on the battlefield for a gateway to victory. The option he took proved to be his biggest mistake.

The Bloody Lane

By the time the sun was up, McClellan had decided to make a frontal attack in a bid to break Lee's center. It was a decision worthy of a World War I general oblivious to the threat to the lives of his men. McClellans's lines of soldiers, protected only by the guns they carried, advanced across an open field to attack the Confederate division of D.H. Hill, which was lined up behind the earth wall of a sunken road. The only way such an assault could ever work was if the attacking force possessed sufficient courage and numbers to withstand punishing fire across open ground. The Northerners possessed both these

Above: *The dead lying on the west side of the Hagerstown Road near David Miller's cornfield, where fighting was severe as the Union army tried to push the Confederates out of their strong position.*

attributes, but they still paid a heavy price in casualties as they closed on the entrenched Confederates. Eventually, Northern numbers turned the balance and the Confederates fell back, but they had not been broken. Northern officers expected reinforcements to help break through, but McClellan gave them nothing, preferring to keep his 20,000 reserves out of the fight. His soldiers' sacrifices had been for nothing; his severely mauled group of men could not press home the attack without fresh support. The advance stalled and the action shifted to the Confederate right flank and perhaps its toughest defenses. McClellan seemed to be digging himself into a grave.

McClellan's attack on Burnside's Bridge across Antietam Creek was intended as a diversion to

stop Lee from shifting all his troops to his vulnerable left flank, but as at Waterloo—when Napoleon sent troops against the farmhouse of Hougoumont—the diversion turned into a draining and bloody assault where neither side would relent. For three hours, Northern troops struggled to take the stone bridge. Eventually, they forced the Confederates away from it and other Northern troops managed to cross the creek further down, but by this time they were exhausted and severely battered. They began to advance on Sharpsburg, but here luck gave Lee his first break.

A.P. Hill's Confederate division had remained at Harper's Ferry to guard prisoners, but now returned to Sharpsburg in the nick of time, plugging the gap in the Confederate right flank. It served to stem the Northern advance by the late afternoon. McClellan, with 20,000 of his own troops still uncommitted in reserve, called off the attack. It had been a disaster. With almost twice as many men as Lee, he had thrown away any chance of victory. He had allowed himself to be

Above: *A dead artillery crew lies outside Dunker Church on the left flank of the Confederate position.*

drawn into prolonged, draining attacks on strong defensive positions, with no positive gain. He had lost 12,400 men. The outcome for Lee was no better, losing 13,700 of his own soldiers, but he had survived the Northern onslaught and retreated unmolested to fight another day.

Below: *The Clara Barton Memorial. Known as the Angel of the Battlefield, she helped to establish the American Red Cross in 1881 after working for the International Red Cross in Europe.*

A CONFRONTATION

Major James Austin Connolly served in the 123rd Illinois Infantry in the Northern Army during the Civil War. In a letter to his wife, he described a confrontation with a Confederate soldier:

"As we were riding along talking, I discovered a Johnnie [Northern slang for a rebel soldier] off to the left of the road, about a quarter of a mile distant, dodging along behind a fence, and running fast toward the mountain: spurring my horse over a low place in the fence by the roadside, and followed by a couple of the escort, we went tearing off over the fields at a rapid rate.

The reb soon found it was no use to run, so he stopped; I reached him first, and he stretched out his hand as if to shake hands with me, the color was gone from his face, he shook as with an ague [fever], and he couldn't utter a single word. He had slipped away from his regiment near Tunnel Hill the night before, and had come home to see his wife, and had started back to his regiment when I caught him.

"He was mounted behind one of my men and we went by where his wife lived, so that she might see he was unharmed and bid him goodbye. Poor woman, I felt sorry for her, and her four little children, as she and they stood around me in tears, entreating me to leave the husband and father with his helpless family. . .but I had to refuse and turn away with my captive, leaving that little family alone among the frowning mountains. . .These are the little tragedies of war more dreadful to me than the larger ones."

GETTYSBURG 1863

A few hours' indecision in assessing the terrain around Gettysburg and seizing the high ground contributed to the defeat of General Robert E. Lee and the Confederate forces. It also lost them their last chance of a decisive victory.

Major General George Meade (1815–72), commander of the Union Army of the Potomac at Gettysburg. Born in Cadiz in Spain, Meade graduated from West Point in 1835 but left the army to become a civil engineer. He re-entered the army in the Corps of Topographical Engineers, and took part in the Mexican War of 1846–8.

The Southern states could not win a long war. If it came to a war of attrition and materials, the North would hold the upper hand. In a bid to even the odds by swift, aggressive campaigning, the South had encouraged its leading general, Robert E. Lee, to invade the North, but his achievements in 1862 (see Antietam) had failed to break Northern resolve. With time running out and in an attempt to encourage the support of a European state, the following year Robert E. Lee took his army of Northern Virginia back on the offensive and threatened the Northern capital with 76,000 men. The North responded by raising 115,000 soldiers and shadowing the Confederate army, but as in the previous year, failed to attack the Southern forces when they were spread out. Perhaps fearing a repeat of the mistakes that led to Antietam, the Northern general George B. McClellan was replaced by George C. Meade. The stage was now set for the greatest battle of the Civil War.

A Rolling Battle

Neither side really expected a major battle; events just dragged them toward it. Robert E. Lee used his cavalry as his eyes and ears. They normally informed him of the enemy's exact position and numbers, but his horsemen had been diverted by a raid, and he was now operating with only a vague sense of a Northern army approaching him. In June 1863 he decided to concentrate his army at Cashtown. Hearing of a supply of much-needed footwear in the nearby town of Gettysburg, a group of Southern riders set out to commandeer the supplies. As they approached the small town, they bumped into the outposts of a Northern scouting group. Shots were exchanged. Rather than retreat, the Confederate forces hung on and forced the Northern troops back into the town. Word spread that a conflict was developing, and more and more troops joined both sides fighting in the town.

By the end of July 1, the Confederate forces had fought a running fight through the streets and forced the Northern troops out of the town. Sensing that if he moved fast, there might be an opportunity to catch the Northern army off balance, Robert E. Lee quickly shifted his whole army south to take control of the town. The Northern forces now made a quick and valuable decision. In order to defend themselves until their whole army could join them, they took up positions on a long spur of high ground overlooking the town. General Meade arrived that night and decided to make his stand on this high ground. By not moving that evening, Robert E. Lee lost the advantage of a rapid attack. At this point, both armies expected a major confrontation on the following day.

On the morning of July 2, Meade's Northern forces occupied the high ground outside Gettysburg from Culp's Hill on its right flank, along Cemetery Ridge in its center, to Little Round Top on its left flank. Lee matched this with troops spread out all along the base of the

General Robert E. Lee (1807–70), commander of the Confederate army at Gettysburg. Also a graduate of West Point and a participant in the Mexican War, Lee became superintendent of West Point before the Civil War. He is widely regarded as the most able of the Civil War generals. The portrait was taken by Mathew Brady, the Civil War's foremost photographer, at Richmond, Virginia in 1865.

*The site where Pickett's
charge came to an end.*

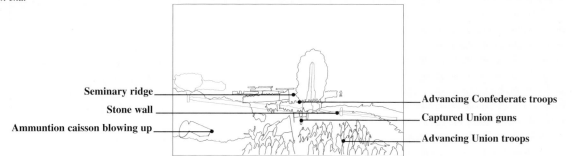

Seminary ridge

Stone wall

Ammuntion caisson blowing up

Advancing Confederate troops

Captured Union guns

Advancing Union troops

The dark blue of the Union forces.

The gray uniforms of the Confederate army.

Sergeant Major Artillery, US Army full dress

Sergeant, Infantry, US Army full dress

Private, US Infantry fatigue marching order

Corporal, Cavalry, US Army full dress

Private, Light Artillery, US Army full dress

Great coat for all mounted men

First Lieutenant, Infantry, CS Army

Sergeant, Cavalry, CS Army

Corporal, Artillery, CS Army

Private, Infantry, CS Army

Infantry, CS Army overcoat

Cavalry, CS Army overcoat

high ground and wasted valuable time by awaiting the arrival of further troops. As his army grew, so did the Northern Army, with more troops joining Meade on the hills. By late afternoon, Lee finally decided to launch an attack. A diversionary assault began on the Northern right flank at Culp's Hill, but his real aim was the Union's supposed weak left flank at Little Round Top. By taking this, Lee hoped to turn in on the Northern center and roll up Meade's army in the classic way.

The Confederate attack began with an artillery barrage, and soon gray-clad lines of soldiers were assaulting Meade's left flank. They overran a group of rocks known as Devil's Den and started the ascent towards Little Round Top. Under pressure from the diversionary attack at Culp's Hill, Meade could not spare sufficient men to reinforce this weak spot. It was then that the battle became not merely a competition of numbers, but depended on the will and spirit of individual men. At the very end of the Northern left flank on Little Round Top stood a group of soldiers, the 20th Maine, commanded by Colonel Lawrence Chamberlain. Chamberlain was an earnest 34-year-old college professor who believed passionately in the Northern cause. His commanding officer told him: "I place you here! This is the left of the Union line. You understand. You are to hold this ground at all hazards!" If Chamberlain failed, his would be the point at which the Northern army would begin to be rolled up to the center. The whole fate of the army depended on his performance.

Chamberlain and his 358 men braced themselves along the wooded, rock-strewn ledge. With the shrill yell of rebel war cries coming up from below, they knew their time had come. Three units of Alabama troops marched up through the trees and rocks to face the men from Maine. A ferocious firefight broke out. "Our regiment was mantled in fire and smoke," recalled Theodore Gerrish. "How rapidly the cartridges were torn from the boxes and stuffed in the smoking muzzles of the guns. How the steel rammers clashed and clanged in the heated barrels. How the men's hands and faces grew grim and black with burning powder." Sensing that even he might be outflanked, Chamberlain spread his men even more thinly so they managed to curve around the right flank of the Confederates, catching them in a withering crossfire. Neither side lacked in courage or will.

The Alabama troops attacked again and again,

Fighting on the second day at Gettysburg, showing the Confederate attack at Cemetery Hill.

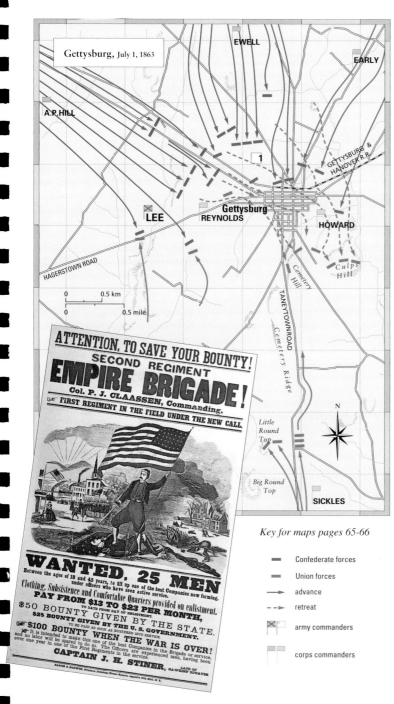

Gettysburg, July 1, 1863

1 *July 1, 5.30 A.M. Opening shots are fired. Confederate and Union forces converge on Gettysburg, with Union forces falling back on Cemetery Hill.*

2 *July 2, 4 P.M. to dusk. Confederates attack and take Devil's Den but Union forces secure Little Round Top.*

3 *5.30 P.M. to dusk. Confederates attacking the Peach Orchard drive the Union forces back to Cemetery Ridge.*

4 *6.30 A.M. until dark. Culp's Hill and Cemetery Ridge attacked by Confederate forces, but very little ground is gained.*

5 *July 3, 5.30 A.M. Continuous attacks on Culp's Hill are ultimately unsuccessful.*

6 *3 P.M. Pickett, Pettigrew and Trimble's infantry advance, suffering huge losses of some 5,600 men.*

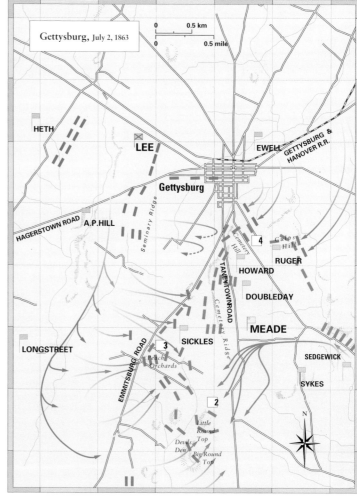

Gettysburg, July 2, 1863

Key for maps pages 65-66

Confederate forces
Union forces
advance
retreat
army commanders
corps commanders

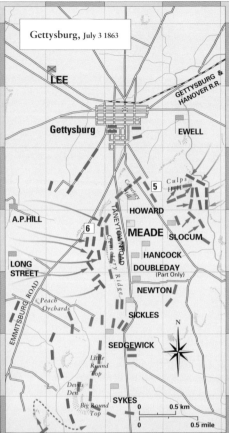

Gettysburg, July 3 1863

LEE

Gettysburg

EWELL

GETTYSBURG & HANOVER R.R.

Culps Hill

5

HOWARD

A.P.HILL

6

MEADE

SLOCUM

HANCOCK

LONG STREET

DOUBLEDAY
(Part Only)

TANEYTOWN ROAD

Cemetery Ridge

NEWTON

EMMITSBURG ROAD

Peach Orchards

SICKLES

N

SEDGEWICK

Little Round Top

Devils Den

SYKES

Big Round Top

0   0.5 km

0   0.5 mile

stumbling under the hail of fire, but rallying and charging again up the hill. Where Confederate troops managed to meet his line, fierce hand-to-hand fighting took place with bayonets, rifle butts, fists, and rocks. "At times I saw around me more of the enemy than my own men," recalled Chamberlain, "gaps opening, swallowing, closing again with sharp convulsive energy." But the men from Maine would not be shifted. Even Chamberlain's younger brother was not spared the full force of the fighting, and was used to plug a gap. Short of ammunition and with a third of his men lying dead or wounded, Chamberlain decided to go for a do-or-die effort. As soon as he shouted the order "Bayonet!" the surviving soldiers of Maine yelled their approval and surged on down the hill. It was too much for the Alabama soldiers to bear. The screaming tide of blue-clad soldiers broke the Confederate lines and sent them reeling backwards, finishing off their resistance with volleys of fire. Chamberlain had preserved the left flank as instructed and with it the fate of Meade's army.

Elsewhere on July 2, the Confederates fared better. Both in the center, on Cemetery Ridge, and on the right flank on Culp's Hill, the Southern troops fought extremely hard against the determined resistance of the Northerners. They gained a few local successes, but these were not enough to shift the weight of the battle against Meade. By nightfall, both sides retired hurt and weary. During the night, further Northern reinforcements brought an end to Meade's inferiority in numbers. The Confederate cavalry had returned from their raiding, and it was the argument of their commander, J.E.B. Stuart, that defined the next day's tactics.

Formless skirmishing began the day on July 3 as Lee gathered his men for the next big attack. Having failed to turn either flank, he now decided on a grand Napoleonic assault, throwing over 15,000 men forward in a penetrating attack on the center of Meade's army, aimed at splitting

Pickett's Charge on the third day of the battle, painted by Thure de Thulstrup.

the Northerners in two. It was a daring and bold move, but one that took little account of the ferocious firepower now existing on the battlefield. Although George E. Pickett was only one of four divisional commanders involved, this assault would forever be named after him, perhaps in an attempt to remove responsibility for it from the revered Confederate commander.

Pickett's Charge

The attack began at 1 P.M. with a massive Confederate barrage from almost 140 cannons. For two hours, the artillery bombarded the Northern central position along Cemetery Ridge. Meade, however, had anticipated this attack and drawn units from his line to reinforce his center. Among these he placed several cannons in hidden positions. By the middle of the afternoon, the terrific cannonade ceased, and lines of gray-clad soldiers emerged out of their wooded positions and began to assemble in formations advancing towards Cemetery Ridge. They made an awesome sight, over 15,000 of Lee's finest troops all pledged to defend the Confederate cause. Lewis Armistead was one of the brigade leaders, and he set off with his men across farmland, through fields of wheat, past two farmhouses, and onward to the Northern line. Northern cannon began to open up on them, throwing cannonballs that scythed down lines of soldiers, but the Southerners marched on for over a mile. Then a thunderclap of musket fire raked through their lines, making them falter as though walking into a storm. Meade's hidden artillery opened up, catching the ragged lines of attackers in a murderous crossfire. One Confederate flag fell ten times, only to be picked up again and again. Armistead pierced his hat with the end of his sword and held it high in the air. "Come on boys!" he shouted to the men behind him. "Give them the cold steel! Who will follow me?" The

stone wall on Cemetery Ridge was their objective, and the remaining Confederate soldiers yelled back, showing their determination to reach it. They paid a terrible price for bravery.

Only Lewis Armistead and 150 men clambered over the stone wall to confront the Northern soldiers in their own position. This moment of supreme bravery has been called the "high water mark" of the Confederate army, for never again would their cause come so close to victory. But it was not nearly enough. Meade threw in his reserves and the Confederate breakthrough was annihilated. Lewis Armistead placed his hand on an abandoned cannon, but within moments he was cut down by Northern bullets. Thousands of Southern bodies lay strewn across the battlefield. Lee now feared a devastating counterattack, but it never came. Meade's army was as exhausted as his. When Lee finally slipped away, Meade made little effort to pursue him, for which he was later criticized. Each side had lost approximately 23,000 dead and wounded soldiers.

Although Lee had not been crushed by the defeat at Gettysburg, it did mark the last chance of victory for the Confederate cause. The war dragged on for two more years with Northern armies turning the tables and penetrating deep into Southern territory. The importance of Gettysburg was readily understood at the time,

More men fought and died at Gettysburg than in any other battle on North American soil.

not only for its strategic implications but also for the tremendous loss of life. Just four months after the battle, Abraham Lincoln visited the site and gave his famous speech in which he spoke of the "new birth of freedom" brought by this terrible war and set out the terms of a "government of the people, by the people, and for the people." As politicians were to realize in later wars, such enormous sacrifices by ordinary people brought with them a responsibility and greater need for democracy to reflect these individual contributions to a nation's survival.

The occasion on which Lincoln gave the Gettysburg Address was the creation of the Gettysburg National Cemetery. As in previous battles fought around the world, the bodies of the dead had been hastily thrown into a common grave; but now, such was the significance of this battle and the war in general, that it was decided to re-bury these bodies in a formal cemetery. This created the model for many other cemeteries of remembrance throughout the United States. The battlefield has been preserved as a Military Park, and a visitor center and panoramic tower provides detailed information about the disposition and movement of troops in the battle.

RORKE'S DRIFT 1879

Few battles illustrate better than Rorke's Drift the value of a thoughtfully prepared position. Its dogged defense by a tiny contingent of well-disciplined troops was reflected by the highest number of Victoria Crosses ever awarded in a day.

Rorke's Drift Victoria Cross winner Lt. John Rouse Merriott Chard of the Royal Engineers. Chard hailed from Devon, England, and had served in Bermuda before his posting to Africa. On his return to England, he was invited to Balmoral by Queen Victoria who gave him a gold signet ring. He later served in Cyprus, India, and Singapore. After contracting cancer of the tongue, he died in Somerset in 1897, aged 50.

The Battle of Isandlwana shook the British Empire to its core. What should have been a simple imperial victory over a native army—a triumph of Western rifles and artillery over native spears and shields—turned into a nightmare of defeat in which 1,334 British and 470 African allied soldiers were slaughtered by a force of ferocious Zulus. The battle that followed this combat at Rorke's Drift has since become a legend of survival against overwhelming odds.

The Washing of the Spears

After absorbing the Republic of South Africa into its empire, Britain inherited the Boer border dispute with Cetewayo, king of the Zulus. A martial race of black tribesmen, the Zulus had invaded southern African territory, easily overwhelming the indigenous people. The guns of the white Boer settlers had brought a halt to these conquests, but the Zulus were far from happy when Britain now sought to bring them under control.

The Imperial forces in South Africa were under the command of Lieutenant-General Lord Chelmsford, who had only seen action in India and Abyssinia. In 1879, he led an army of 5,000 British and 8,200 native troops into northern Natal. They crossed the Zulu border, marked by the Mzinyathi river, and prepared for the campaign by converting an isolated mission post at a place known as Rorke's Drift into a military base. One of the buildings was used as a hospital and the other one became a store for ammunition and food. Chelmsford then divided his army into three columns and started an organized search for the Zulu army. However because the Zulus were ready and waiting they came upon the British first.

At Isandlwana, beneath a dramatic outcrop of rock, Chelmsford's central column set up camp. Early in the morning of January 22, at the height of the South African summer, some 10,000 Zulu warriors emerged out of the long grass and flung themselves at the 3,000-strong British army. Equipped with repeating Martini-Henry rifles and backed up with artillery, the British should have had the best of it, but the Zulus were an experienced fighting force. Although some Zulus were armed with European rifles, most wielded deadly assegai spears, used for both throwing and stabbing. Initially inflicting heavy casualties on the advancing warriors, the British force was too thinly spread to stem the main attack.

The Zulus adopted their usual bull's-head formation with the horns of their army sweeping around the flanks and rear of the defenders. The British were unable to form a strong defensive position and found themselves broken up into small groups of desperate men. Angered by the casualties inflicted on them by Western firepower, the Zulus gave no mercy and swept over the camp, killing everything before them—British and native soldiers, horses and camp pets, even spearing store boxes and wagons. Each defeated enemy was stabbed many times and their stomachs were slit open as the Zulus

Cetewayo, king of the Zulus, was born c. 1827 and had a deep suspicion of both Europeans and Boers. Cetewayo defeated his rival half-brother in a bloody battle in 1856, thereby securing his right to the throne. He became king from 1873 until his death in 1884.

*The view of Rorke's Drift
from the Oskaberg.*

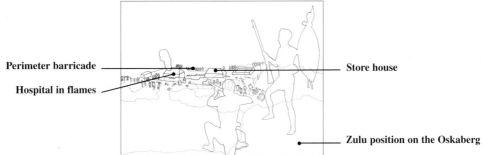

Perimeter barricade

Hospital in flames

Store house

Zulu position on the Oskaberg

During the Battle of Isandlwana, officers Teignmouth, Melvill and Coghill struggle to save the Colors of 1st Battalion. Both men died in the attempt. The tattered remains of the colours were found a fortnight after the battle, and are now in Brecon Cathedral. A painting by Alfonse de Neuville in 1881.

to this was a surgeon and three men of the Army Hospital Corps taking care of 35 sick people. Lieutenant John Chard, a subaltern of the Royal Engineers, had been left in command of the base. A decision had to be made quickly: Should the tiny garrison flee or stand? A group of veteran Zulu warriors was on its way toward them commanded by Prince Dabulamanzi kaMpande. They had not taken part in the fighting at Isandlwana and were eager for a victory of their own.

A Desperate Situation

Having fought courageously at Isandlwana, the men of the Natal Native Horse were in no mood to stay at Rorke's Drift. Chard implored them to stand by him, but they had had enough. The British were furious, and some fired shots at them as they rode away. Having no horses themselves and only able to transport the wounded and sick in slow, cumbersome wagons, the British began to realize they had little choice but to remain at the base. They quickly had to turn the mission post into a fort.

There were two main buildings: The hospital and storehouse. Loopholes were knocked into the walls of the buildings so that riflemen could shoot from inside. A considerable pile of mealie bags and cracker boxes were dragged out of the store and used as sandbags to create an improvised wall around the perimeter of the base. The one weak point was the high ground overlooking base known as the Oskarberg. However, the buildings backed on to it and so gave limited protection to the defenders from any firepower situated there.

At 4.30 P.M. on the afternoon of January 22, some shots were heard to the south of Rorke's Drift. An impi (regiment) of some 4,000 Zulu warriors was fast approaching. Moments later, a British lookout shouted, "Here they come, black as hell and thick as grass!" The impi swung

believed this let the spirits of the dead escape. The Zulus had bathed their spears in the blood of the invaders and were hungry for more.

The handful of survivors who fled Isandlwana streamed back to the Zulu border. A group of black horsemen known as the Natal Native Horse rode to the military base at Rorke's Drift and gave them news of the dreadful defeat. The post was guarded by Lieutenant Gonville Bromhead and 80 men of B company of the 24th Regiment (Foot), made up largely of Welshmen. In addition around to the rear of the outpost. Zulu skirmishers armed with rifles took to the high ground, while wave upon wave of Zulu warriors in close formation charged forward, bristling with assegais and shields. Huddled inside the post buildings, riflemen of the 24th opened fire, each one of their shots taking a casualty in the mass of bodies before them. Stung by the hail of fire, the impi drifted around to the front of the hospital where they overran the garden and began to pound against its doors and windows. Inside

Below: *A Zulu in visiting dress, Uyedwana at Issikobosa Kraal. Painted by G.F. Angus in 1847.*

Above: *Jim Rorke's house at Rorke's Drift after the battle in 1879, with the Oskaberg behind it.*

the hospital, soldiers of the 24th were placed among the sick and wounded, and those patients who were fit enough and could handle a gun were given one.

The soldiers in the hospital put up a good fight but the sheer weight of numbers outside forced them out of the front room, and the Zulus broke in. Fortunately, there were no interconnecting corridors between the rooms, and the soldiers in the front room escaped by making a hole into the room beyond. They defended this hole with rifle fire and bayonets until other soldiers had made a further hole behind them in order to evacuate the patients into another room. From room to room, the soldiers fought a desperate battle with the Zulus, spears stabbing through the holes in the plaster, one man defending the hole while others hacked at the walls behind to escape. Finally, they broke into the fortified compound behind the hospital. The Zulus were unable to penetrate further, and they eventually set fire to its dry thatched roof.

The Zulu skirmishers on the Oskarberg continued to fire into the compound. Athough armed with rifles less effective than the Martini-Henry, they nevertheless kept the garrison pinned down and inflicted casualties on the soldiers defending the front of the post who had their backs to them. Riflemen at the rear of the post dueled with them effectively, but again the sheer weight of numbers was wearing them down. Lieutenant Chard decided to reduce the size of the perimeter and ordered his men to take cover behind a wall of cracker boxes outside the front of the storehouse. Wounded soldiers such as Corporal Allen and Private Hitch helped all the patients out of the burning hospital to the new defensive line.

It was evening now, but the darkness brought no rest as the Zulus surged around the buildings right up to the tight ring of defenders. Mealie bags were dragged across to raise the height of the defensive wall. The Zulus were at the very

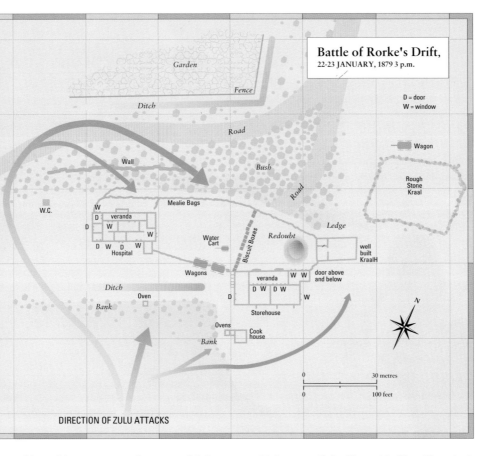

Battle of Rorke's Drift,
22-23 JANUARY, 1879 3 p.m.

D = door
W = window

Wagon

Garden

Fence

Ditch

Road

Wall

Bush

Road

Rough
Stone
Kraal

W.C.

Mealie Bags

Ledge

W
D   veranda
D   W
W

Water
Cart

Biscuit Boxes

Redoubt

well
built
KraalH

D W D   W
Hospital

Wagons

veranda   W W   door above
and below

Ditch

Oven

D W D W

Bank

D   W

Storehouse

Ovens

Bank

Cook
house

N

0   30 metres

0   100 feet

DIRECTION OF ZULU ATTACKS

*Rorke's Drift Victoria Cross
Winner Lt. Gonville
Bromhead who commanded
"B" Company of the 2nd
Battalion 24th Regiment.
Bromhead was outranked by
Chard when it came to
commanding the tiny forces
at Rorke's Drift. Despite the
deafness which had
handicapped his military
career, Bromhead was
allowed to continue in the
service. He died in Allahabad
in 1891 at the age of 46.*

base of it, and bayonets proved more useful than rifle shots. It was desperate hand-to-hand fighting. Waves of warriors leapt over the bodies of their companions to stab and thrust at the British. Only an hour before dawn did the fighting begin to peter out. When the sun rose, the British saw hundreds of Zulu bodies stacked against the wall of cracker crates, some piled as high as the barricade itself. Thousands of cartridges littered the ground. Fifteen of Chard's men were dead, and almost all of them were wounded. Fearing another assault, Chard sent men out to gather any weapons they could lay their hands on, Zulu assegais included. When the bullets ran out, they

would have to fight like with like. They had barely grabbed arms full of spears when they were recalled into the compound. The Zulus had returned, and this time the British feared it was for the final blow. Bracing themselves for a last stand, they saw the Zulus gather on a hill opposite the post. The mass of warriors crouched on the ground and stared down at the redcoats. They had had enough. Fighting nonstop for almost twelve hours, the Zulus could see little point in carrying on. Standing up, they turned their backs and left the brave little garrison behind. It was a wise decision. Lord Chelmsford and the remainder of his army were returning to Rorke's Drift, and

The defense of Rorke's Drift, from a painting by A. de Neuville.

with that the British were saved. The heroic defense of Rorke's Drift has entered into military history as one of the truly great feats of survival. It helped mask the disaster of defeat at Isandlwana, and, gave time for Lord Chelmsford to consolidate and launch a successful counterattack. Eleven Victoria Crosses (VCs), were awarded to the defenders: Lieutenants Chard and Bromhead, Surgeon Major James Reynolds, Acting Commissariat James Dalton, Corporal William Allan, Privates Frederick Hitch, Henry Hook, Robert Jones, William Jones, and John Williams (all of the 24th), as well as a Natal Volunteer, the Swiss Friedrich Schiess, who although a patient, fought boldly. This was the highest number of VCs awarded in a day. Six months later, the British dead were avenged by the defeat of the Zulu army at Ulundi. The Zulus suffered heavy casualties and their king, Cetewayo, fled, and was captured by the British.

Reconciliation

Today, Rorke's Drift is a thriving community. Thirty-one miles (50 km) away from the nearest Natal town of Dundee, it is still isolated. Though the original buildings of the mission post were destroyed, two structures were raised on their foundations, one of which closely resembles the hospital and now houses a battlefield museum. Behind the buildings is a cemetery for the British. The landscape at Rorke's Drift and Isandlwana is largely unchanged. In a spirit of reconciliation to lay the ghosts of the conflict, in 1997 descendants of the British and Zulu warriors who fought at Rorke's Drift attended a ceremony in which the Royal Regiment of Wales was twinned with the 121st South African Infantry Battalion.

GALLIPOLI 1915

The invasion of the Dardanelles was supposed to be a bypass around the deadlocked Western Front, an entry into the vulnerable underbelly of the Central Powers. But the campaign turned into one of the war's greatest disasters.

Sir Ian Hamilton (1853–1947), standing second from right prior to taking up his command in Gallipoli. He had distinguished himself in the South African War of 1899–1902 and went on to become military attaché with the Japanese during the Russo-Japanese War of 1904–5. On Hamilton's right is the naval commander Admiral de Robeck.

In 1915, when fighting on the Western Front had become bogged down in the stalemate of trench warfare, the British sought to open a second front in southern Europe by striking at Germany's ally, Turkey. The year-long campaign on the Gallipoli peninsula degenerated into one of the greatest military disasters of all time. The experience is one still vividly recalled by the Australians and New Zealanders who received their baptism of fire there.

Failures in Planning

The Gallipoli campaign began with sound intentions. Shortly after the outbreak of war, Turkey had aligned herself with the Central Powers. Turkey's move derived from her century-old fear of Russian designs upon the Dardanelles Strait, the gateway out of the Black Sea. By the end of 1914, the Allies desperately needed a way to break the Western Front deadlock. Winston Churchill, the 39-year-old First Lord of the British Admiralty, became convinced that the solution was to strike at Turkey, with a view to linking up with Russia.

The Dardanelles looked like a soft target. Guarded only by poorly armed forts along the Gallipoli peninsula to the north, it looked as if it would fall to a naval action alone. When British and French battleships attacked in February 1915, however, three ships were sunk and another three damaged by unsuspected mines. Just when the defending Turkish and German troops were close to collapse, the British commander withdrew, advising that any progress would need to involve the army.

Back in London, the war council came to a similar view, and it was decided that land forces should join the fighting. Although the army's long-term aim was to strike up the River Danube, their immediate purpose would be to help the navy consolidate gains in the Dardanelles. Moreover, as Lord Kitchener, the British Secretary for War, pointed out, there were troops already close at hand; raw recruits from Australia and New Zealand were stationed in Egypt and could easily be redeployed.

Both Australia and New Zealand, though now self-governing, had entered the war in support of Britain. Many still felt a powerful sense of patriotism toward the mother country, and the war

Mustafa Kemal (1881–1938), leader of the Turks' 19th Division, was the inspiration behind the Turkish success at Gallipoli, which earned him the honored title of "pasha." After the war, through further military campaigns, he abolished the sultanate and became the first president of the newly founded Turkish republic. In 1934 he took the name of Kemal Atatürk.

Right: *The landing of the Royal Hampshire Regiment from the River Clyde onto the Gallipoli peninsula.*

also offered a chance for the fledgling nations to make a mark on the international stage. In September 1914, a joint New Zealand and Australian force had set out to Britain for training. Halfway through their journey, however, London ordered them to disembark in Cairo to continue training there. It was also announced that they were henceforth to be known as the Australian and New Zealand Army Corps, a name soon reduced to its famous acronym, Anzacs.

Following the failed naval operation in February, the scheme to use the Anzacs was swiftly developed. Plans for a Mediterranean Expeditionary Force (MEF) were hurriedly drawn up, and a commander appointed—Sir Ian Hamilton. He was a poet, novelist, and hero of the Northwest Frontier and the Boer War. Details, Hamilton was

told, would come later. Meanwhile facts were few; before their departure on March 13, Hamilton's staff even had to scour bookshops for guidebooks to Constantinople.

Hamilton, based in Alexandria, was then told of a change in plan. He was now to lead a combined operation with the navy backing the army rather than vice versa. But no one, it seemed, had thought through the needs of a land invasion such as reinforcements, guns, ammunition, and food.

Meanwhile, the chance of an easy Allied victory had been lost. The Turks, who had foreseen defeat only a month earlier, guessed that a land attack was imminent, and set up a separate army under a German commander, Liman von Sanders. Viewing the cliffs and hills along the Gallipoli Peninsula, von Sanders must have prayed for a

week's grace. In fact, he got a month. In that time, he brought up six divisions, comprising 84,000 men—six times the strength of the original garrison. The troops were well dispersed, linked by good roads, and ready to move fast wherever the landings came. To add to the Anzac's misfortune, the Turks had one particularly brilliant commander in Mustafa Kemal, later the founder of the Turkish Republic. Moreover, the Turks were inspired by patriotic zeal: They were fighting for the defense of their homeland.

A Doomed Landing

The MEP—comprising British and French troops, as well as Anzacs—was 75,000 strong. The amphibious operation they were to attempt

was a difficult one, taking place on beaches backed in many places by cliffs. The plan was to seize the peninsula's high ground a few miles inland. The Anzacs would take the northern sector, a beach adjoining a headland, Gaba Tepe. From their battleships and cruisers, they would be taken to land by a flotilla of "tows"—12 towing boats, each with three barges. The British would concentrate on the Cape Helles Point, the headland that overlooked the entrance to the Dardanelles. No one properly acknowledged the threat posed by the Turks, who were widely dismissed as inferior in every way.

In the early hours of April 25, still remembered as Anzac Day, 11 transports arrived off the 15-mile (24 km) stretch of coast. In the northern sector, the Anzacs began their landing. At once, they were in trouble. In the darkness, the leading tow veered off course and all the others followed. By the time they reached the beach, in what came to be called Anzac Cove, they were in entirely the wrong place, bunched together and in confusion, hemmed in by scrub-covered escarpments. In the grey light of dawn, the 500 defending Turks opened fire. As the first Australians struggled off the shore toward high ground, Kemal accosted his fleeing troops, turned them around, and rushed up reinforcements.

On the shore, later landings crowded into the first ones, already pinned down by Turkish fire. By early afternoon, the beach was a chaos of 8,000 men, with no command and no objective—soldiers were trapped in a state of utter confusion among the dead and wounded. The tows bringing in fresh troops and taking casualties away were easy targets. Moreover, no one had foreseen this level of destruction. The ships offshore could take just 500 casualties. On Anzac Cove, by the end of the first day alone, there were 2,000. By the

George Lambert's painting of the charge of the 3rd Light Horse Brigade at the Nek on Gallipoli.

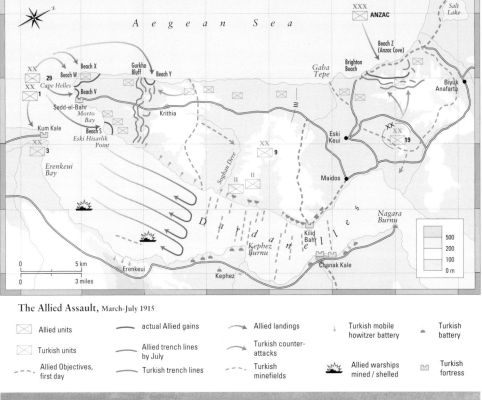

The Allied Assault, March-July 1915

⊠	Allied units	—	actual Allied gains	→	Allied landings	↓	Turkish mobile howitzer battery	▲	Turkish battery
⊠	Turkish units	—	Allied trench lines by July	→	Turkish counter-attacks				
---	Allied Objectives, first day	—	Turkish trench lines	---	Turkish minefields	✸	Allied warships mined / shelled	⊡	Turkish fortress

evening, with 15,000 men ashore, the local commanders began to moot the idea of withdrawal. But Hamilton saw that this would be suicidal—the withdrawing troops would make even better targets. "You have got through the difficult business," he ordered. "Now you have only to dig, dig, dig until you are safe." Hamilton's decision restored morale. There was no more talk of evacuation.

Further south, meanwhile, the main British landing had met with a mixed fate. Thirteen battalions had landed on five beaches on either side of Cape Helles. At either end of the section, defenders were few, but the center was a deathtrap. Slowed by the current, the men landed after dawn and were met by withering fire while they were still in the water. A few survivors made the beach and sheltered beneath a low bank, while thousands more cowered in their landing ship, waiting for dusk. Their colleagues who had landed a mile or two away waited passively for orders to move. No orders ever came.

On the northern- and southern-sector beaches, the Anzacs and British dug in. On the heights above, so did the Turks. Both expected further onslaughts; neither side was in shape to attack. Small-scale assaults were negated by small-scale counterattacks. Both sides held back, building up their strength for a greater battle.

Misery in the Trenches

By May 6, opposing forces on Cape Helles were 25,000 British against 20,000 Turkish. The British chose this moment to attack. They hardly gave themselves a chance of success, however; the assault was ordered with only seven hours' notice, against unknown positions, with few aircraft to observe progress, and without reserves of

ammunition. It failed even to dent the Turkish front. Further assaults achieved nothing but losses, exhaustion, and stalemate. Meanwhile, troops in the northern sector remained locked solid. All

The periscope rifle was invented by an Australian on Gallipoli, here used by a soldier in the 2nd Light Horse Regiment with help from a comrade using a simple periscope.

along the coast, conditions set in that rivaled anything on the Western Front. From their trench positions just beyond the beaches, men were being destroyed by disease, inaction, and appalling, hopeless assaults. The suffering contributed to a new self-image among Australians—that of the tough, independent, irreverent "Digger," a very different character, in the

Antipodean view, from the arrogant, complacent, and class-bound British.

Only after almost three months did the government attempt to break the deadlock, sending another five British divisions to join the seven on the beaches. By then, the Turks had 15 divisions. Hamilton decided on a double blow: a new advance from Anzac Cove, and a new landing at an inlet immediately to the north, Suvla Bay. Both attacks failed. Suvla, in particular, turned into a nightmare for the British attackers. "We lost our leaders early on," wrote a sergeant on one of many fruitless assaults. "I can see them now walking, commanding the approach, smoking, so brave—a fallacy—they were hallmarked by the snipers. . . We were ordered to fix bayonets, another fallacy because the sun glittering exposed our position immediately. It literally became a hell, fire from all angles." By the end of August, this front too was locked solid.

As autumn rains set in and winter frosts claimed their first victims, the British government lost its nerve and ordered an evacuation. The only commendable part of the Gallipoli campaign was the way it ended. Trenches were booby-trapped and rigged to seem fully manned. Guns were fixed to fire automatically, their triggers attached to tins with sand or water trickling into them. On the nights of December 18 and 19, the final 20,000 men slipped away from Suvla and Anzac, undetected. In all, 83,000 had left without a casualty, except for one man who got drunk on rum and drowned. By January 9, Cape Helles was cleared, with equal success.

In the nine months of the campaign at the Gallipoli peninsula, 46,000 had perished on the allied side. They had died for nothing.

SOMME 1916

With the Western Front deadlocked into trench warfare, French and British generals pinned their hopes on a breakthrough by sheer weight of advancing men. Their optimism condemned 20,000 British to death in one day.

July 1, 1916 was a hot day in northeast France. British troops looking across no-man's-land at the Germans dug in on ridges and woodland to the north of the River Somme were full of hope. The first day's objective, the wooded Pozières Ridge, stood out clearly four miles ahead. "The sun was just topping the mist and catching the dewdrops on the grass and thistles around us," wrote Major H. Bidder of the Royal Sussex Regiment. "There was a wonderful cheery air of expectancy over the troops. . . . I have never known quite the same universal feeling of cheerful eagerness."

The contrast between the gentle countryside and the naiveté of the British volunteers made a terrible contrast with what was about to follow—the most intense bloodletting in military history. It would be the greatest single day's loss in the whole war and the birth of several national tragedies, not only for the British, but also for the Dominions—Canada, South Africa, Australia, New Zealand, and India.

The Origins of Folly

The inspiration for the attack had come from the optimistic French commander in chief, Joseph Joffre. He was the senior partner in the Anglo-French alliance and had spoken of a massive breakthrough in an operation between the two allies. The assault therefore had to be at the point where their armies joined, which just happened to

As this painting by an unknown artist shows, the Somme battlefield was a nightmare of shattered trenches, shall-cratered earth, and decaying bodies.

be on the River Somme. But France was bleeding herself into immobility in the defense of Verdun, so the brunt of the assault would have to be borne by Britain. By the summer of 1916, British armies held almost 80 miles (128 km) between Paris and the sea.

The British commander, Sir Douglas Haig, was certain of success. He intended to storm the fortress of German trenches by sheer weight of arms: A long bombardment and a determined advance would cut through the German lines, then "roll up" the Germans between the Somme and the coast. The history of the past year of stalemate on the Western Front was against him. Yet Haig ascribed previous disappointments to a failure to attack firmly enough. For him, success became a matter of blind faith, his mood one of increasing optimism that a decisive result would be forthcoming.

For many months, the future battlefront had been remarkably peaceful. Just to the north of the Somme, high ground had been in German possession since October 1914. Since then, there had been little fighting, marked by a "live-and-let-live" attitude on both sides and fraternization at Christmas. British battalions drilled in full view of the German lines. Behind this veneer, however, the German defenses were formidable.

Haig's plan relied on a massive, sudden artillery barrage to break the enemy's spirit and plough up the barbed wire, the trenches, and the machine-gun posts. For this he had some 1,500 guns, of which 467 were heavy ones—one gun for every 20 yards (18 meters) of front. The second vital element—surprise—was never a possibility, for the preparations had been obvious to the Germans since the previous February. The British plan was further compromised by a divergence of view in the high command: Haig wanted a breakthrough, while others believed that only a limited advance would be possible. The British never had the guns for either, especially one in which the first day's

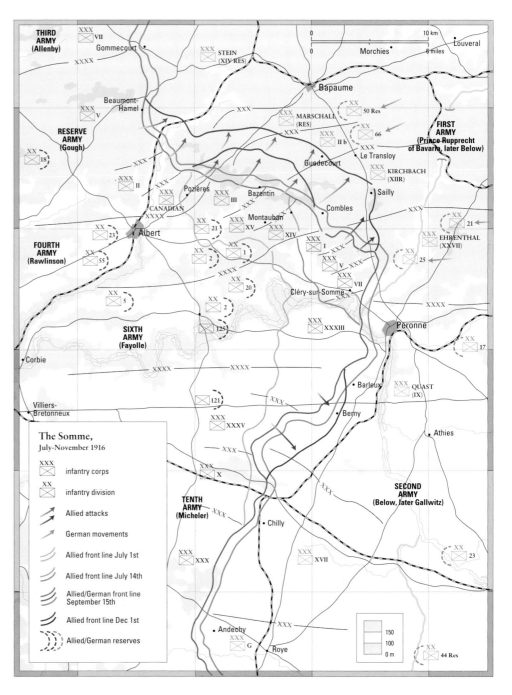

The Somme,
July-November 1916

infantry corps

infantry division

Allied attacks

German movements

Allied front line July 1st

Allied front line July 14th

Allied/German front line September 15th

Allied front line Dec 1st

Allied/German reserves

objective was a ridge that gave a good view of the British advance.

Over the Top

In the last week of June, as two million men faced each other on a 30-mile (48-km) front, the British on their 13-mile (21-km) front opened a massive artillery barrage. They fired off over a million rounds, dumping 20,000 tons of metal and explosive on the German lines, and creating a roar heard on the Downs beyond the Channel over 100 miles (160 km) away.

Much of this turned out to be completely useless. The guns were distributed evenly along the front, with no effort to target their shells on weak points. Many guns were obsolete, lobbing shells that could not penetrate the German dugouts or gun-emplacements. Thus the prime aim of the barrage—to allow an infantry advance—was not achieved. Yet the infantry were sent forward just the same.

Their only hope was to cross no-man's-land before the barrage lifted to new targets further back in the German lines. It was, at best, a race with death. But racing was impossible. For one thing, every man was burdened with 66 lb (30 kg) of gear—between one-third and one half of body-weight—over ground that was a morass of mud and craters. Moreover, the men were to advance at "a steady pace," in lines as neat as ninepins, and just as vulnerable.

When the men, riding the final wave of the barrage, went over the top at 7 A.M., they advanced shoulder to shoulder in waves 100 yards (91 meters) apart. Ahead, the barrage of falling shells lifted. The front-line Germans sheltering in their dugouts dragged out their machine guns and raked the British infantry as if in a fairground shooting gallery. At the same time, undamaged German guns rained down artillery shells.

"We never got anywhere near the Germans," recalled Corporal W. Shaw of the Royal Welch Fusiliers later. "Our lads was mown down. You couldn't do anything. The machine-guns were levelled and they were mowing the top of the trenches. The officers were urging us on, saying, 'Come on lads, follow the flash!' [of color on the back of an officer's collar]. But you just couldn't. It was hopeless. And those young officers, going ahead, that flash flying in the breeze, they were picked off like flies." All that was left of the advancing British were pockets of men cowering in shellholes. However, there was progress, of a sort, in the south. The French, straddling the Somme itself on an 8-mile (13 km) front, moved forward with only small losses—partly because their advance was less rigid, partly because the Germans had focused on the British.

In the British sectors, every assault led to a bloodbath, even when the troops made ground. In one extreme case, the 752 men of the 1st Newfoundland Regiment suffered 684 killed or wounded (91 percent) in just over half an hour. By noon, about 100,000 men had gone over the top—20,000 of them were killed and another 37,000 wounded.

That evening, at rollcall for the 14th platoon of the 1st Rifle Brigade, which had been 40 strong that morning, only one man answered; the other 39 were dead. The one success—by the 36th Ulster Division penetrating for 2 miles (3.2 km) past Thiepval—bogged down in failure when no reserves backed them up, leaving them isolated and divided.

In this sector, the British took just over 500 prisoners, and less than 2,000 along their whole front. The French, along their much smaller front, took 4,000. By the evening of the first day, the British had advanced just over a mile (1.6 km) at best. Day after day, for two weeks, they hammered at

To keep the army supplied, a horse team brings up artillery shells through a lake of frozen mud.

British machine gunners in gas masks pose for the camera on the Somme in July 1916.

had been in preparation for a year. The first, "Little Willie," was built in 1915. Haig needed something to break the deadlock, but the tanks were not yet ready for use and kept breaking down. Of the 60 that had arrived, 49 went to the front, and 32 went into action, but only 9 actually advanced with the infantry. They amazed all who saw them.

"What in the world was it?" wondered a film-maker, Geoffrey Makins. "For the life of me I could not take my eyes off it. The thing—I really don't know how else to describe it - ambled forward with slow, jerky, uncertain movements. . . . It waddled, it ambled, it jolted, it rolled, it—well, it did everything in turn." Certainly, the sight shocked the Germans. "They felt quite powerless against these monsters which crawled along the top of the trench enfilading it with continuous machine-gun fire." Delville Wood and High Wood were taken at last; another mile gained. But a high price was paid for revealing the war's greatest secret weapon.

The last attack was in mid-November. The British had advanced at most 5 miles, but so slowly that the German lines had been rebuilt as strong as ever. The British and the Dominions had 420,000 casualties, the French 200,000, and the Germans 450,000. In the words of A.J.P. Taylor, "The Somme set the picture by which future generations saw the First World War: brave helpless soldiers; obstinate generals; nothing achieved."

Today, the countryside is peaceful once again. Those who dash along the highways to Reims or Lille hardly see a sign of the struggle. Only those who explore the minor roads can find the hidden scars—the mounds, the exposed trenches, white graves amidst the corn—that recall the place where a million men were killed or wounded.

the German lines, with nothing to show but another two miles of mud and thousands more killed and wounded.

The Extended Battle

In mid-July, the commander of the British 4th Army, Sir Henry Rawlinson, suggested an attack on a 4-mile (6.4-km) front, aiming at spots on the ridge marked by Delville Wood and High Wood. He proposed to use novel tactics: a night-time advance and a quick bombardment. Initially, these worked. On July 14, 20,000 men swept over the German lines. High Wood was briefly cleared with a charge by Indian cavalry. Then came a German counterattack and High Wood was lost again. The attack on Delville Wood itself was horrific. It was borne by the South African Brigade of 3,150 men. For five days they fought, often hand-to-hand. When relief came only 758 were left. The attacks continued through August, degenerating into a war of attrition.

Now that the idea of a breakthrough had gone forever, Haig should have called a halt; but he had promised a great victory, and could not—would not—stop. If there was to be no breakthrough, Haig opted for "methodical progress." This meant steady battering on Pozières Ridge against an immovable force. In one sector, held by the Anzacs—the Australian and New Zealand Army Corps—23,000 men were killed or wounded to gain a mile of mud. Australians were appalled at what they saw as murder by an incompetent, callous, and deluded leadership.

Another assault on September 15 relied on a new invention: The tank, a secret weapon which

CAMBRAI 1917

In a war of futile attrition, the battle of Cambrai raised the prospect of a break in the stalemate of the Western Front. The first mass use of the tank marked a turning point in warfare and the use of terrain, once commanders realized its potential.

Field-Marshal Paul von Hindenburg (1847–1934), the German commander in chief (left), confers with his strategist, General Erich von Ludendorff (right) and the Kaiser, Wilhelm II (centre). Hindenburg relied on Ludendorff's abilities as chief of staff, the two ruling Germany as virtual dictators.

The sight across the gently rolling landscape around Cambrai, in northeast France, on November 20, 1917, astonished both the British attackers and their enemies. Almost 400 tanks, operating en masse for the first time, loomed out of the early morning mist, "looking like giant toads" to one British corporal. They bore on their snouts huge bundles of brushwood. These odd, lumbering machines with their enigmatic burdens were to be the magic weapon that would cut through lines against which the British infantry had cast itself in vain for three years.

The Roots of Success and Failure

The year of 1917 had been terrible for the British and her allies on the Western Front. There seemed no way to break the dreadful stalemate of trench warfare, no way to burst through the fortress of defenses created by the Germans, no way to break the thinking of conservative commanders, to avoid ineffective bombardments, or to prevent even more men marching in line abreast across no-man's-land, facing machine guns.

The arrival of the tank—prematurely, and in small numbers—on the Somme in September had lit a light in the darkness. The tank's origins lay in

a need for something that would move, fire, and protect all at once, like a battleship on land. This necessity was matched by a new invention already having some success on muddy fields: A tractor that ran on caterpillar tracks. The link between the two was made by Colonel Ernest Swinton after seeing the trenches in October 1914. He proposed a vehicle that would be "capable of destroying machine-guns, of crossing country and trenches, of breaking through entanglements, and of climbing earthworks."

Of Britain's leaders, only Winston Churchill, then First Lord of the Admiralty, proved receptive to Swinton's ideas. The War Office and senior officers, still imbued with a mystical belief in the virtues of cavalry, were against it. Under Churchill's aegis, the first committee was formed to study what were then called "land-ships." The word "tank" had not yet been invented—it came along later as an innocuous codeword for the strange objects. Their naval origins are still recalled by residual nautical terminology—even today, tanks have "hulls."

The trials of the first tank, nicknamed "Little Willie," were held in February 1916, and 150 were ordered. These machines, weighing about 30 tons and measuring some 26 feet (8 meters) long, could cross an 11-foot (3.3-meter) trench. They could crawl at walking pace and had a range of 24 miles (38 km). Their suspension was terrible, which meant that tracks tended to break after about 50 miles (80 km). Each one took a crew of eight, including a brakeman for each track and a

The British Third Army commander, General Sir Julian Byng (1862–1935), was one of the inspirations behind the use of tanks. His plans were compromised by delays that ate up the reserves vital for a successful tank assault. After the war, he was governor general of Canada for five years.

Anti-tank artillery fire

Armament on the
sides of the tank

Barbed wire entanglements

First line trenches of the
German Siegfried Line

Cambrai, NOVEMBER – DECEMBER, 1917

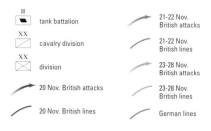

tank battalion	21-22 Nov. British attacks
cavalry division	21-22 Nov. British lines
division	23-28 Nov. British attacks
20 Nov. British attacks	23-28 Nov. British lines
20 Nov. British lines	German lines

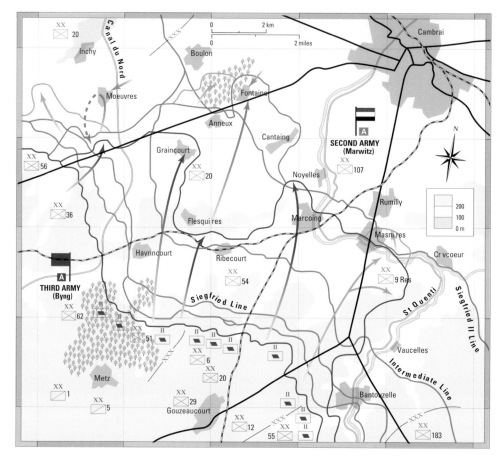

navigator who steered by compass with two heavy wheels dragging behind like a rudder. The crew was trained in a secret enclosure near Thetford, Norfolk. Once ready, the tanks were to be used in a surprise attack.

It was not to be. In September 1916, 60 tanks were shipped out to the Somme, where the British were mired in one of the costliest and most fruitless attacks of the war. A few of them, thrown into action prematurely, helped the British to a small

Spearheaded by advancing tanks, the British gained an unprecedented 5 miles (8 km) of ground. English machinegunners relax in a moment of calm in a captured trench at Ribecourt.

advance, but in doing so they revealed the weapon that should have remained a secret.

The conservative, ever optimistic commander in chief, Sir Douglas Haig, still scorned the tank as a "minor factor," and so did many other officers. But the commanders of the new Tank Corps saw its potential. In August 1917, while British and Dominion troops were dying in the swamps of Passchendaele, the Tanks Corps commanders suggested a raid near Cambrai, 50 miles (80 km) to the south, into rolling land well-drained by two canals. The aim would be to surprise the enemy with silence and speed. There would be no pre-liminary bombardment. The tanks would destroy, demoralize, and get out quickly after three hours, without capturing ground. Haig was still eager for victory in Passchendaele and postponed the idea. Only in the autumn, when the notorious mud of that battlefield had swamped Haig's ambitions, did he accept it.

With time, the plan grew in scale, backed by the Third Army commander, General Sir Julian Byng. But it still retained two crucial elements: the tanks and the lack of an opening bombard-ment. The tanks would spearhead a breakthrough between the two canals beyond the Hindenburg Line to seize the town of Cambrai, take rising ground marked by a village, Flesquières, and by Bourlon Wood, then speed onwards towards Valenciennes, 25 miles (40 km) to the northeast. To cross the forbidding German defenses—known to them as the Siegfried Line and to the Allies as the Hindenburg Line, after the German commander in chief—the tanks would carry huge bundles of brushwood, known as "fascines," to fill in the trenches.

This was a basis for genuinely new tactics. Behind the tanks, in single file—not in line abreast—would come the infantry to mop up. The two elements, tanks and infantry, would advance together in close support of each other, the tanks opening the way, the infantry following close

Germans were confronted by this metal monster which was invulnerable to machine-guns and grenades, and could straddle trenches.

behind to defend them from close-quarter attacks.

The plan also laid the foundations for failure. This was now to be a major offensive and would need reserves. But by the time the plans were approved, with an attack planned for November 20, all the reserves had been absorbed elsewhere.

Otherwise, preparations were meticulous. "We have done all our marching by night and hidden ourselves by day," wrote Captain George Samuel of the Royal Field Artillery to his fiancée. "No fires have been allowed—in fact it has almost been a crime to show an electric torch at night!" Feints with gas, smoke, and dummy tanks deceived the Germans, a deception completed when—without the bombardment which had

always preceded an attack in the past—the 381 real tanks went in along a 6-mile (9.6-km) front.

The Attack

Only in one spot did they hit trouble. Near the center, around Flesquières, the conservative General Harper of the 51st Highland Division doubted the efficacy of the new machines, so he set off an hour after everyone else simply because he did not believe the Hindenburg Line would be crossed so quickly. The delay gave the Germans time to bring up field guns. Then Harper allowed his tanks and infantry to spread out too far, with the result that German machine gunners and

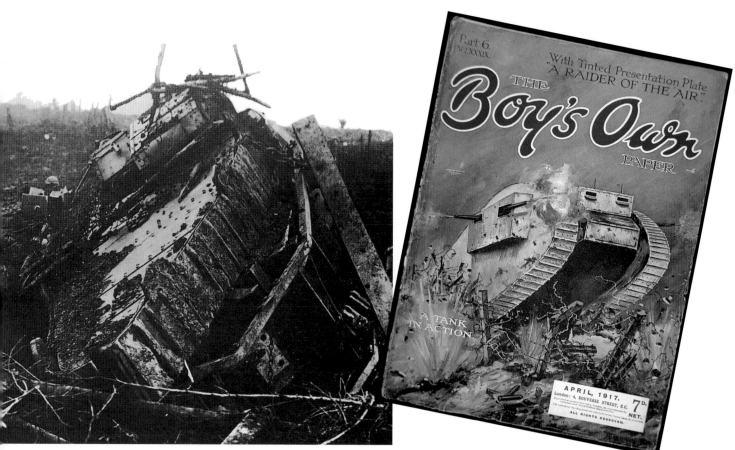

The promising success of the few tanks that had seen premature action on the Somme in September 1916 encouraged some to see the new machines as a weapon that could win the war.

The first tanks moved at walking pace and were hard to maneuver. This one was put out of action after falling into a shell-hole.

artillerymen could focus on tanks and infantry in turn. The tank crews worked desperately at their cumbersome controls to drive a zig-zag course, and the gunners tried to return fire. But taking accurate aim while pitching, tossing, and turning was virtually impossible. One by one the tanks were hit. Those crew members who were not killed outright burned to death.

Afterwards, reports suggested that one German artillery post knocked out several tanks, though no-one was sure. Certainly, five burned-out hulls were found later, but British rumors—enthusiastically supported by Harper himself—soon spoke of a single German artilleryman destroying 16 tanks, a legend seized upon by pro-cavalry officers as "proof" of the tank's inadequacy.

In fact, everywhere else, the tanks and infantry had sliced quickly through the three German lines by midday, bypassing the blockage at Flesquières and advancing for up to 5 miles (8 km), to the very edge of Bourlon Wood. Never had there been such a success on the Western Front. George Samuel's reaction reflected the general elation: "Six hours pure joy. ... Think of the hundreds of 'tanks'—think of the hundreds of guns—all got up quietly and secretly and let loose at the Hun without a thing to warn him of coming trouble. I can't get over the wonder of it."

The advance was the equivalent of a month's heavy fighting on the Somme or in Ypres, where the killed and wounded numbered in the tens of thousands. By contrast, killed and wounded on the first day at Cambrai were 1,500, against 10,000 prisoners taken and 200 guns seized. When the news reached London, church-bells rang in celebration for the only time in the war.

But then came delay for the whole afternoon. While the Germans rushed in reinforcements to block the gap, there were no British reserves to leapfrog the exhausted attackers. British commanders were apparently as surprised by the tanks' success as the Germans were by it. A cavalry charge, slowed by barbed wire and rough going, fell easy prey to German machine guns.

The next day, the attack continued. The British managed to take Flesquières, advancing another 1.5 miles (2.4 km) to take the village of Fontaine-Nôtre Dame, only to lose it again a day later. Over the next nine days, front-line pockets, including the shattered and abandoned Fontaine-Nôtre Dame, were won and lost several times.

Meanwhile, the Germans had been gathering their reinforcements. There were signs that they were about to retaliate; a large number of German reconnaissance planes flew over British lines, while British planes were driven away by shellfire from places where the enemy forces had concentrated. But the signs—reported by local officers on the ground—were ignored by commanders still elated by the initial advance.

On November 30, it was the Germans' turn to attack. Without making an initial bombardment, and behind screens of gas and smoke, fresh German infantry infiltrated the exhausted British in their weakly held lines and seized gun emplacements, forcing the British to retreat. Some 6,000 British were taken prisoner. Within a matter of days, all the ground that had been won was lost again.

At home, the elation of the success ten days before gave way to depression. An official enquiry turned out to be one of the war's most notorious whitewashes. It reported that the setback was entirely the fault of those who could not

Germans maneuver a field gun during the counterattack that recaptured all the ground they lost during the Cambrai offensive.

answer back—junior officers and the dead. The commanders were blameless. To say anything else would have undermined public confidence in the military leadership.

All that was left was the knowledge of what tanks and infantry could achieve when correctly and responsibly used. That knowledge helped the British when on August 8, 1918, 456 tanks at last broke through the German lines, driving the Germans toward surrender. The German military leaders told their parliament, the Reichstag, that it was the tank above all that made further resistance impossible. Without Cambrai, allied victory would have come, if at all, in a very different, and probably far bloodier way.

Looking back, Winston Churchill considered the needless slaughter on the Western Front, and asked a rhetorical question: what else could be done? "I answer, pointing to the battle of Cambrai, 'this could have been done,' and would have been done, if only the generals had not been content to fight machine-gun bullets with the breasts of gallant men."

PEARL HARBOR 1941

The attack on Pearl Harbor by a carrier-borne force of torpedo- and fighter-bombers was carried out with complete surprise. Neither country was at war, and various warning signs were ignored, with catastrophic results.

Admiral Isoroku Yamamoto (1884–1943) had not been in favor of war with the U.S., but once it was inevitable, he advocated a pre-emptive knock-out strike. Later put in charge of naval operations in the Solomon Islands, Yamamoto was shot down by U.S. fighters over Bougainville on 18 April 1943.

At dawn on Sunday December 7, 1941, the destroyer U.S.S. *Ward* was patrolling the entrance to the U.S. naval base of Pearl Harbor on the Hawaiian island of Oahu. On watch, Lt. William Outerbridge spotted the conning tower of a midget submarine in forbidden waters. He gave the order to open fire, and the submarine sank. When he reported the incident, another patrol boat was ordered to investigate. That was all. No one suspected the little sub's significance: it was one of five midget subs launched from larger submarines probing in advance of the Japanese fleet less than 300 miles (480 km) away. Aboard its aircraft carriers, Japanese fighters were preparing for the attack that would define the course of the war.

The Path to War

Tension had been building for over a year. Japan, which had had a mainland empire in Manchuria since 1931, had built up a formidable fleet and had made bold claims to a Pacific empire. In 1940, she allied herself with Germany and Italy. In response, President Roosevelt had ordered the U.S. Pacific Fleet to the base of Pearl Harbor. With Germany's successes in western Europe, Japan looked hungrily toward French and Dutch territory in southeast Asia, eager for rich deposits of oil and rubber in the Dutch East Indies to fuel

her expansion. Without those resources, Japan's 253 warships, 3,000 planes, and massive army would soon be immobilized. When in July Roosevelt froze Japanese assets in the U.S., Admiral Isoroku Yamamoto, Commander in Chief of the Japanese Combined Fleet, became convinced that war was inevitable. He was determined to strike first.

It was a bold venture. Yamamoto was a talented naval strategist, Harvard-educated, with a good understanding of U.S. power. He was sure the only way to secure victory was to neutralize the U.S. presence in the Pacific with one swift blow. He was inspired by an attack by old-fashioned British Swordfish planes carrying torpedoes, which sank three Italian battleships in Taranto harbor in November 1940. Americans thought Pearl Harbor was too shallow for such an attack, but the Japanese had copied new British designs that allowed torpedoes to be launched in 40 feet (12 meters) of water. Torpedo-bombers, then, would spearhead the assault, which would come on a Sunday, America's day of rest. In Yamamoto's scenario, the U.S. would rally, but meanwhile Japan would have had time to fortify her new empire with a ring of bases.

The key to this strategy was secrecy. The Japanese fleet had to sail for 12 days to get Japan's fighters within striking distance, and the

Admiral Husband E. Kimmel, commander of the U.S. Pacific Fleet at Pearl Harbor, and one of the men later blamed for the disaster

Pearl Harbor on the south coast of Oahu

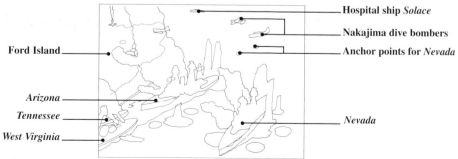

Hospital ship *Solace*

Nakajima dive bombers

Anchor points for *Nevada*

Ford Island

Arizona

Tennessee

West Virginia

Nevada

ships had to travel undetected. To cover the plans, Japan unleashed a flurry of misinformation. The fleet's departure from the Kurile Islands on November 26, accompanied by an easily detected exchange of coded messages, was hidden by a blizzard of fake radio transmissions. In Washington, Japanese envoys continued spurious negotiations until the very day of the assault. A luxury liner set off for an ostensibly peaceful cruise to San Francisco, but with secret orders to turn around at midnight on December 6.

The strategy worked. Despite intelligence reports of an impending attack, U.S. commanders believed the Japanese would fall first on southeast Asia. So the Japanese fleet of 6 carriers with 22 support vessels and 3 submarines remained undetected on that dark and moonless pre-dawn some 230 miles (368 km) north of Hawaii. At 6.00 A.M. the first wave of aircraft took off: 40 low-level torpedo-bombers (Nakajima B5N2s,

known as "Kates"), another 50 high-level "Kates," 50 "Val" dive-bombers, and 50 "Zero" fighters. A second wave of 170 bombers took off an hour later.

Tora! Tora! Tora!

Two-and-a-half hours later, U.S. radar operators spotted a large blip on their screen. They thought it must be American B-17 bombers on their way from the U.S. Then, outside the harbor, the *Ward* depth-charged another of the five midget submarines trying to get through. Again, no one ashore suspected real trouble. In the vast harbor, all was quiet: attended by about 90 smaller ships, seven of the fleet's eight battleships lay at their jetties along "Battleship Row" (the eighth was in dry dock). On the *Nevada*, at the northern end of the row, marine bandsmen were preparing to play for the raising of the flag

A Japanese photograph shows Ford Island at the beginning of the raid. A "Kate" peels off after scoring a direct hit on the Oklahoma.

at 8.00 A.M. Only now did the duty officer report the odd incidents with the submarines to Admiral Husband Kimmel, commander in chief of the Pacific Fleet, in his home above the harbor. Meanwhile, the Japanese strike force, flying south at over 9,800 feet (3,000 meters), were high above thick clouds. On his radio, the Japanese commander, Lt. Commander Mitsuo Fuchida, heard Hawaian music from Honolulu, and knew he was nearing his target. Spotting a gap in the thick cloud cover, he led his planes down to follow Oahu's coastline, planning to swing in from the south. About the time Kimmel received his call, the Japanese peeled off to attack, some aiming at the airfields, but most heading for the harbor.

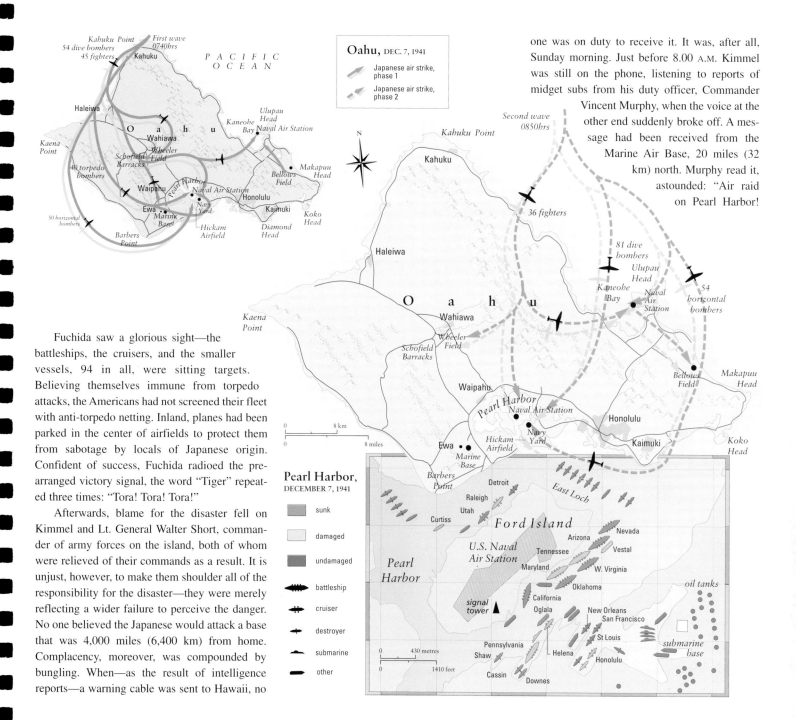

Oahu, DEC. 7, 1941

Japanese air strike, phase 1

Japanese air strike, phase 2

Kahuku Point
First wave 0740hrs
54 dive bombers 45 fighters
Kahuku

PACIFIC OCEAN

Haleiwa

Kaena Point

O a h u
Wahiawa
Wheeler Field
Schofield Barracks

Ulupau Head
Kaneohe Bay
Naval Air Station

40 torpedo bombers
Waipahu
Pearl Harbor
Naval Air Station
Ewa
Marine Base
Navy Yard
Hickam Airfield

Bellows Field
Makapuu Head

Honolulu
Kaimuki
Koko Head

50 horizontal bombers
Barbers Point
Diamond Head

Second wave 0850hrs

Kahuku Point

Kahuku

N

36 fighters

Haleiwa

Kaena Point

O a h u
Wahiawa

81 dive bombers

Ulupau Head
Kaneohe Bay
Naval Air Station

54 horizontal bombers

Schofield Barracks
Wheeler Field

Bellows Field
Makapuu Head

Waipahu

Pearl Harbor
Naval Air Station

Honolulu

Hickam Airfield
Navy Yard
Ewa
Marine Base

Kaimuki

Koko Head

Barbers Point

0   8 km
0   8 miles

Fuchida saw a glorious sight—the battleships, the cruisers, and the smaller vessels, 94 in all, were sitting targets. Believing themselves immune from torpedo attacks, the Americans had not screened their fleet with anti-torpedo netting. Inland, planes had been parked in the center of airfields to protect them from sabotage by locals of Japanese origin. Confident of success, Fuchida radioed the pre-arranged victory signal, the word "Tiger" repeated three times: "Tora! Tora! Tora!"

Afterwards, blame for the disaster fell on Kimmel and Lt. General Walter Short, commander of army forces on the island, both of whom were relieved of their commands as a result. It is unjust, however, to make them shoulder all of the responsibility for the disaster—they were merely reflecting a wider failure to perceive the danger. No one believed the Japanese would attack a base that was 4,000 miles (6,400 km) from home. Complacency, moreover, was compounded by bungling. When—as the result of intelligence reports—a warning cable was sent to Hawaii, no

one was on duty to receive it. It was, after all, Sunday morning. Just before 8.00 A.M. Kimmel was still on the phone, listening to reports of midget subs from his duty officer, Commander Vincent Murphy, when the voice at the other end suddenly broke off. A message had been received from the Marine Air Base, 20 miles (32 km) north. Murphy read it, astounded: "Air raid on Pearl Harbor!

Pearl Harbor, DECEMBER 7, 1941

sunk

damaged

undamaged

battleship

cruiser

destroyer

submarine

other

East Loch

Detroit
Raleigh
Utah
Curtiss

Ford Island
U.S. Naval Air Station

Nevada
Arizona
Vestal
Tennessee
Maryland
W. Virginia
Oklahoma

Pearl Harbor

signal tower

California
Oglala
New Orleans
San Francisco

St Louis

oil tanks

submarine base

Pennsylvania
Shaw
Cassin
Downes
Helena
Honolulu

0   430 metres
0   1410 feet

This is no drill!" Kimmel dropped the phone and ran out to see for himself. Japanese "Kates," zooming in at 100 feet (30 meters) to release their torpedoes, struck five battleships: the *California*, *Oklahoma*, *West Virginia*, *Arizona*, and *Nevada*. The *Arizona* exploded when a direct hit down her funnel blew up a magazine, while the *West Virginia* escaped capsizing only because of prompt counter-flooding to re-balance her. Then, from higher up, bombs hit the remaining two, *Maryland* and *Tennessee*. Men leaped overboard into water already coated with thick oil, which caught fire and consumed many of them.

The airfields were also caught by surprise. At Fort Shafter, 8 miles (13 km) inland, men had formed lines for breakfast and watched astonished as the Japanese Zero fighters zoomed in for the attack. They had no notion of danger until the machine guns opened up, cutting down dozens. On Wheeler Field, Hickham, and Kaneohe naval air stations, planes soon became burning wrecks. In half an hour, Fuchida led his planes back out toward their carriers.

Meanwhile U.S. pilots and gunners had rallied, in time to face a second wave of 170 bombers and fighters. In the harbor, dive bombers again struck the *Nevada* as she struggled out to sea, then turned on the drydocks. The *Pennsylvania* was shielded by billowing smoke, but the dry-docked destroyer *Shaw* was blown apart when a

Survivors from the West Virginia *are rescued from her burning hulk.*

magazine exploded. By 10.00 A.M. it was all over, and by 1.00 P.M. the Japanese force was safe, with the loss of just 29 planes out of 360. They left behind them fearful destruction and a population in panic. *West Virginia* was listing; *Arizona* had broken in two and capsized, taking 1,000 trapped men to their deaths; *Oklahoma* had turned turtle, ramming her masts into the mud; and *California* had settled on the bottom, down to her superstructure. Thirteen other smaller vessels were damaged or sunk, and 188 planes—including most of the U.S. seaplanes—were destroyed. At sea, five aircraft from the incoming carrier *Enterprise* were shot down by their own nervous gunners. In all, some 2,400 men had been killed.

Disaster Leads to Victory

At first, Pearl Harbor seemed a masterstroke, the key to an advance that by May 1942 would take Japan across all of southeast Asia, Dutch East Indies, and New Guinea, to the very shores of Australia. With hindsight, however, the attack was unnecessary. If the Japanese had attacked the Philippines, Borneo, and Java—as originally planned in the summer of 1941—the U.S. Pacific Fleet could have done little to retaliate, and Japan would have secured much of the territory and raw materials she sought.

Tactically, the attack was less damaging than it seemed. Pearl Harbor's dockyard installations and oil supplies were largely left intact. Only four battleships were sunk. In an age when carriers now dominated strategy, two U.S. carriers, *Lexington* and *Enterprise*, were out of the harbor, and remained untouched. Even the damage done was reparable—*Nevada* later took part in the Normandy invasion and the battle of Iwo Jima. Five other battleships were repaired in time for the invasion of the Philippines three years later. More to the point, the attack instantly turned the

Above *Caught by the second wave of attackers, the magazine of the drydocked destroyer* Shaw *explodes.*

Right *The front page of the* Los Angeles Times. *A radio station in the city warned of imminent invasion; thousand of armed men flocked to the Hall of Justice in response.*

U.S. from a nation struggling to keep the peace into a country on the brink of war. Until then, many remembered the horrors of the First World War and questioned the wisdom of becoming embroiled in a second. Now there was no question: the surprise attack was perceived as ruthless, perfidious, and unforgivable. Stunned disbelief was followed by fury and some panic—San Francisco declared a state of emergency, fearing invasion. Thousands besieged recruiting offices. Pearl Harbor united the American nation and the future Allies as no other act could have done. President Roosevelt, announcing war the following day, told a cheering Congress that December 7 was "a date that will live in infamy." Britain declared war on Japan the same day. There could be no rest until she had been defeated.

The strategic and tactical blunder was compounded by one of the most disastrous political miscalculations in history. Japan called on her ally Germany to join in the war against the U.S. Until that moment, the U.S. had no specific reason to fight Hitler, for Germany was bound by treaty only to come to Japan's aid in the event of a direct assault on her. But Hitler could not resist matching the Japanese bravura. Besides, he was sure that the U.S. would declare war on him, and he wanted to be seen to move first. "We will always strike the first blow!" he told a cheering Reichstag, and at 2.30 P.M. on December 11, the American *chargé d'affaires* in Berlin was told that "Germany considers herself to be at war with the United States."

Within four days, a largely European struggle had become a true world war. Since there was no realistic possibility of Japan or Germany occupying the vast and untapped reserves of the United States, the attack on Pearl Harbor virtually guaranteed the defeat of both countries.

El Alamein 1942

Thanks to numerically superior forces and Allied domination of the German and Italian supply routes, General Montgomery won the decisive battle of the North African campaign, opening the way for the British/US invasion of Italy.

General Bernard Montgomery (1887–1976), in the Royal Tank Regiment beret he habitually wore. His flare for publicity endeared him to his troops, but often infuriated his superiors. A professional soldier since serving in the Royal Warwickshire Regiment during the First World War, Montgomery went on from Africa and Italy to become commander of the land forces in the Normandy invasion of 1944.

El Alamein, no more than a small town on the coast of Egypt, gave its name to one of Europe's great decisive battles during the Second World War. To the survivors of this great desert contest, the name evokes grim memories of appalling heat, sandstorms, and deprivation. To strategists, it represents one of the war's mightiest confrontations. It was a clash not only between two vast tank armies but between two of history's most colorful personalities: General Erwin Rommel, known as the "Desert Fox," and his adversary, Montgomery— "Monty" to his adoring troops.

North Africa in the Balance

Italy had entered the war in June 1940, hoping to seize North Africa and the British-held Suez Canal. Instead, they had been soundly defeated, allowing British forces to pose a threat to Germany's advance into Greece. To extinguish that threat and save his unreliable allies, Hitler sent in General Erwin Rommel, the dashing, resourceful tank officer who had distinguished himself in the invasion of France. In a brilliant advance, Rommel pushed the British back to the Egyptian border, thus threatening Britain's position in the whole eastern Mediterranean. In late June 1942, Rommel was on his way to Cairo and Suez. If Suez fell, Rommel would be free to sweep on through the oil-rich Middle East and join up with German forces in Russia. It was not to be, however. Sixty miles (96 km) from

Alexandria, at the little coastal town of El Alamein, the British Eighth Army under the command of General Sir Claude Auchinleck made its stand in early July 1942. During that month, in a battle that became known as "First Alamein," the two sides fought each other to a standstill. It was time to finally break the Desert Fox, and Churchill had just the man to do the job: Lt. General Bernard Montgomery.

There was a new urgency to this mission and new hope as well, for on July 25 the U.S. and Britain had decided on a master plan to invade Europe through North Africa. An invasion of northwest Africa was planned for early November and was designed to squeeze Rommel between two armies. Montgomery took command just at the moment when resources, strategy, and supremacy in the air combined to give him the best possible chance of success.

Montgomery was something of a wild card. An unconventional, eccentric man, he had never commanded large masses of armor. But he was brilliant and ruthless, with an obsessive personal commitment to the struggle. He kept a picture of Rommel on the wall of his caravan, along with a quotation from Shakespeare's *Henry V*: "O God of battles! Steel my soldiers' hearts." And he knew well the power of publicity, always wearing a black beret to make him instantly recognizable. "That beret is worth two divisions!" he claimed.

Rommel's next attack, at the end of August, was blunted by the loss of supply ships to Allied planes based in Malta. The Germans had only 203

General Erwin Rommel (1891–1944) was, like Montgomery, a professional soldier who had first seen service during the First World War. His striking early successes over the British Eighth Army in North Africa earned him the sobriquet of the "Desert Fox." When it became evident in 1944 that he had condoned the attempt on Hitler's life, he was given the choice of court martial and firing squad or suicide. He chose to die by poisoning himself.

tanks against 767 British and failed to break through, withdrawing after a week. Over the next six weeks, both sides prepared for the battle that would decide the fate of North Africa, and thus the outcome of the planned Allied invasion.

Rommel knew he was unable to rely on superiority of forces. The two Panzer divisions at the heart of his Afrika Korps may have been without equal, but out of his 100,000 troops, 50,000 were Italian—the very men whose failures had brought him to North Africa in the first place. Furthermore, only half his new supplies were getting through the Allies' naval and air blockade. So Rommel changed the rules: He abandoned a war of movement for one of defense, creating a 40-mile (64-km) line unprecedented in desert warfare. It ran along the high ground of the Miteirya Ridge, blocking the way between the sea at El Alamein and the impassable marshes of the Qattara Depression.

The key to Rommel's defensive line was a complex of minefields 5 miles (8 km) deep that the Germans called "The Devil's Gardens." Among the half-million mines were notorious S-mines—which would leap into the air and explode at waist height—and Teller mines, which would withstand the weight of an infantryman but would explode beneath a truck or tank. The mines were cunningly laid with carefully plotted "freeways" designed to lead attackers into a maze from which there would be no way out.

Meanwhile, Montgomery had built the Eighth Army into a vastly superior force—almost 200,000 men and over 1,000 tanks, together with 2,300 guns and 530 planes. On every count this amounted to about twice the numbers of Rommel's army. Monty's was a mixed force, with Australians, New Zealanders, Indians, South Africans, and even some Free French and Greek brigades, which he made uniquely his own. In particular, he set about welding rival branches—infantry, tanks, and air power—into a single

force. Moreover, Monty had scores of new American Sherman tanks with 75mm guns and high explosive shells that could knock out German anti-tank guns at long range. They were far more of a match for the Panzer IVs than some of the older British tanks, such as the Valentine.

Force alone would be no use against mines, however. Fortunately the Eighth Army could take advantage of the newly invented mine detector, a device that when swept back and forth above the ground would emit a high-pitched whine when passed over metal. Five hundred were available at El Alamein. In addition, "Baron" tanks made out of obsolete Matildas were fitted with chain flails that detonated mines in their path. Monty was taking no chances. While building up his armed forces, he also ordered that a dummy army base be built along the southern sector of the front — complete with a fake pipeline, railway, trucks, dumps, and even cardboard soldiers. Meanwhile, in fearful heat and maddening sandstorms, his men constructed their own well-camouflaged base in the north.

But it was the skill of the British codebreakers that delivered the final coup. Not only did they reveal Rommel's supply problems, but they also uncovered a stroke of luck. In September, Rommel fell ill with jaundice and high blood pressure and returned to Vienna for treatment. His replacement, the codebreakers revealed, was to

A motorcycle and sidecar combination of one of the Africa Korps' Panzer Divisions. Such reconnaissance units were major contributors to the flexibility that made Rommel such a formidable opponent.

Australians advance warily on German positions through a dense smoke screen on November 3, 1942, the day before the Allied breakthrough.

be Lt. General Georg Stumme, a veteran of the Russian front inexperienced in desert warfare.

Attack and Stalemate

The attack, codenamed "Lightfoot", opened on the evening of October 23. Beneath a full moon, the silence was shattered by the thunder of 1,000 British guns and the rumble of tanks by the hundred. The tanks blasted a way forward for the sappers, who gingerly opened routes into the minefields, marking them with tape and hooded lanterns. One Australian major later recalled that as the infantry followed the barrage through a pall of smoke, "the ground vibrated under our feet just like the skin of kettledrums." The main thrust of the attack, comprising tanks and infantry with fixed bayonets, focused on a 4-mile (6.4 km) stretch near the coast, while a diversionary attack took place at the southern end of the German line.

All night, the British cut through the minefields. They continued throughout the following day and night. It was a slow, dangerous process, with a traffic jam of vehicles constrained in narrow lanes and exposed to German shells. The

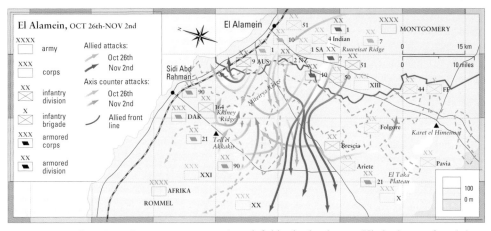

Allied success forced the Germans to go on to the counterattack, but they now faced a well-established wedge of British armor. By the evening of the second day, the defending 15th Panzer Division had lost three-quarters of its tanks—but had succeeded in stalling the British advance. The chance of an Allied breakthrough was lost.

Meanwhile, fate had again dictated change on the German high command. The day after the attack opened, General Stumme was blown from his car by a burst of fire and his bemused driver

left him in the desert. (His body was found days later; he had died of a heart attack.) Late on the 24th, Rommel, convalescing near Vienna,

Below left: *A formidable German 88mm gun in action. This weapon, designed as an anti-aircraft gun, was fearsome when used in ground warfare. It could knock out a tank at a range of 6 1/4 miles (10 km).*

Below: *A German shell explodes a safe distance away from a British tank.*

In a painting by Terence Cuneo, the 2nd Battalion, the Rifle Brigade fight off the German assault on Kidney Ridge, October 27, 1942.

received a telephone call from Hitler. "The news from Africa sounds bad," the Führer said. "No one appears to know what has happened to General Stumme. Do you feel capable of returning to Africa?" Rommel did not hesitate. He was back at El Alamein the next evening.

Over the next two days (the 26th and 27th), the stalemate focused on a hillock, Kidney Ridge (thus named by the British because of its shape). German and Italian tanks assaulted it four times without success. The fifth attack was met by a massive bombing raid; for two hours British planes dropped high explosives on a pocket of land only 3 miles (4.8 km) long by 2 miles (3.2 km) wide. The Germans were forced back, but the British failed to create a way forward.

General Montgomery, combining supreme self-confidence with flexibility, rapidly drew up another plan; with infectious bravado he code-named it "Supercharge." First he switched the direction of the advance northwards; then, when that too was stalled by a rush of German armor, he recommenced the assault from Kidney Ridge. On the night of November 2, Supercharge began, but the British and their allies once again found themselves mired in minefields; by dawn they had become sitting targets for German guns. By nightfall, they had lost another 200 tanks.

Both sides were near despair. Rommel ordered retreat, but received an extraordinary counter-mand from Hitler: "Yield not a meter of ground. Your enemy, despite his superiority, must also be at the end of his strength." That night, the 3rd, Rommel wrote to his wife Lu: "I haven't much hope left. At night I lie with my eyes wide open, unable to sleep for the load that is on my shoulders." Even Monty was beginning to doubt ultimate victory, while his superiors—in particular, Churchill—were becoming anxious that Rommel would survive to fight off the Allied invasion planned for only four days later.

In fact, the Allies were nowhere near the end of their strength. Rommel had only 55 tanks left—and falling—while the Allies had over 600, and rising. Allied losses were appalling: For each tank lost by the Germans, the Allies lost four. In the end, it was sheer weight of arms—combined with the confusion of the canceled retreat—that prevailed. It was a tribute to Rommel's genius that the Germans held out for so long.

Breakthrough to Victory

The breakthrough came soon after dawn on November 4. Allied infantry—51st Highlanders and the 5th Indian Division—cut a gap between the Afrika Korps and the Italians. With the possibility that the British would cut off his retreat, Rommel at last received the permission he sought, and pulled back. Some 50,000 Germans lay dead, versus Monty's losses of 13,500.

The German retreat became something of a rout, but Rommel managed to hold his depleted force intact. For two days, the coast road was crammed with German troops, tanks, and staff cars, all in wild confusion as Allied planes strafed them. Monty failed to overtake them and cut them off, however. His advance was slowed by his caution—and by a rainstorm on the 6th that turned the desert into a morass.

Rommel, in a series of brilliant rearguard actions, with only 10 tanks left, fell back, losing all the territory he had once gained. Little towns that had become famous when the Germans were advancing—Sidi Barrani, Tobruk, Benghazi —fell to the British one by one, until Tripoli itself, Germany's main supply base, was within reach.

It took another six weeks to reach Tripoli. The Allies finally entered the city on January 23, only to find that Rommel had pulled out by sea, destroying the harbour's installations. Meanwhile, the Allied army that had landed as planned in Morocco and Algeria in November was thrusting eastwards. The two Allied forces met in April 1943, and the road to Europe —via its "soft underbelly," Italy—was open.

STALINGRAD 1942–3

The failure of the Germans to take this industrial city in a siege lasting six months marked the turning of the tide in the southeast of the Soviet Union. Hitler had underestimated the ability of the Red Army to use the city's natural defenses.

General Friedrich von Paulus (1890–1957) became a captain in the First World War and helped to plan the German invasion of Russia. The terrible number of German casualties at Stalingrad was due in part to Paulus's code of honour, which prevented him from disregarding Hitler's futile commands. As a prisoner, Paulus did a volte face and helped to organize resistance to the Nazis.

On August 24, 1942, Stalingrad seemed on the brink of collapse. The previous evening, German tanks—the spearhead of the Sixth Army—had clattered through the northern suburbs to the banks of the River Volga. To their south, beneath a pall of smoke, lay a city already devastated by earlier German bombing. That evening, as another 600 planes turned the central area to rubble, dive-bombers strafed refugees as they crowded the ferries crossing the river. Within two days, 40,000 people had died.

A Flawed Plan

Stalingrad's fall was intended to be the culmination of a brilliant advance. The previous winter, Hitler's invasion of Russia had been stalled. Then, in July, he had launched a summer offensive of staggering ambition, aiming to seize southern Russia, roll on southward through the oil-rich Caucasus and the Middle East, and join with German armies in North Africa. By the end of August, the German front reached from the shores of the Black Sea almost to the Caspian.

This grandiose strategy was fatally flawed, however. The German armies were overstretched, and the Russian buildup beyond the advancing front line was far greater than Hitler suspected. He then undermined his own plans by focusing on Stalingrad (present-day Volgograd). Although Stalingrad was important as a center for rail and river transport, it was only in late July (after the main Caucasus offensive had been launched) that

Hitler decided it should be a target. This strategy in itself became compromised when Hitler transferred one of the attacking Panzer (tank) armies away from the city, only changing his mind yet again. By then it was too late to take the poorly defended city by surprise.

In any event, Stalingrad was not the easy target Hitler supposed. Straggling for 20 miles (32 km) along the Volga's precipitous western bank, divided by the steep gorge of the Tsaritsa River, this grim industrial city was well positioned for defense. To the east, across the Volga, was the immensity of the Russian steppes, where Russians could build up forces untouched. And Stalingrad was of special significance for Russia's dictator, Joseph Stalin: He had commanded the place, then named Tsaritsyn, in the 1919–21 Civil War, and renamed it in his own honor. Now, finding his city under siege, he gave an order: "Not a step backwards!" The struggle for Stalingrad was to become both personal to Stalin and the very crux of the war in the east.

Following Stalin's orders, the city set about its defense. Every able-bodied man was conscripted, including 7,000 teenage boys. Three lines of defense protected the factories, the squat government buildings, the two railway stations, and the 330-foot (100-meter) knoll known as Mamayev Kurgan. To the north, a Russian army stood in reserve. For two weeks, the German general General Friedrich von Paulus, commander of the Sixth Army, hesitated to launch what should have been a final assault. Fearing to expose his men to

Marshal Georgi Zhukov (1896–1974) served briefly in the Tsarist cavalry before joining the Red Army in 1918. By 1941 he was Stalin's Chief of General Staff and became a national hero for his relief of Moscow that year. He went on to capture Warsaw and Berlin, and accepted the German surrender on May 8, 1945.

a possible Soviet counterattack, he let valuable time pass by.

By this time the Russians had begun to recover under Stalingrad's new commander, General Georgi Zhukov, hero of the previous winter's defense of Moscow. His secret strategy was a high-risk one, and brilliant. Stalingrad would be kept alive, but no more than that, in order to tie down German forces long enough for reserves to build up outside the city. Then the trap would be sprung. Meanwhile, General Vasily Chuikov had been appointed to head up the defending 62nd Army. Though he had a mere 55,000 men and was faced with an enemy numbering over 100,000, he was just the man to turn these odds in his favor. On September 12, the day of his arrival, he assured his superiors: "We shall hold the city, or die there."

Chuikov's appointment came just in time, for on the 13th, three infantry divisions and four Panzer divisions attacked. They reached the very heart of the city, and in places penetrated through to the banks of the Volga. The arrival of 10,000 Russian reinforcements across the river saved the city from collapse, creating a precarious balance.

Street Warfare

Now Chuikov came into his own. Volatile, abrasive, and often brutal, he nevertheless won respect by sharing the privations of his troops. He certainly knew how to get the best out of them. Over the next two months Chuikov turned his men into urban guerrillas, teaching them to create "killing zones," mined areas of ruins through which only the defenders knew their way. They fought for every room of each shattered building: Floors were front lines, and stairways no-man's-land. Often, the Russians returned at night to

German troops batter their way forward in street fighting.

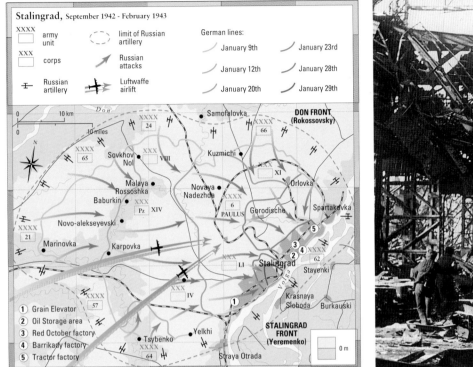

Stalingrad, September 1942 - February 1943

XXXX army unit

XXX corps

Russian artillery

limit of Russian artillery

Russian attacks

Luftwaffe airlift

German lines:
January 9th
January 12th
January 20th
January 23rd
January 28th
January 29th

① Grain Elevator
② Oil Storage area
③ Red October factory
④ Barrikady factory
⑤ Tractor factory

Many of Stalingrad's factories were reduced to ruins of twisted metal during the fighting that raged around and in the vast complexes.

reoccupy old positions, picking their way through the rubble on feet padded with cloth, carrying spades sharpened, to double as weapons. "We sensed and heard the enemy soldiers' breath and footsteps," wrote a Russian, "but we could not see them in the smoke. We fired at sound."

For the Germans, Stalingrad became a nightmare. Endless days and nights of hand-to-hand struggles took their toll. "The street is no longer measured in meters but in corpses," wrote one officer, "and when night arrives, one of those scorching, howling, bleeding nights, the dogs plunge into the Volga and swim desperately to gain the other bank. . . Animals flee this hell . . . only man endures." Chuikov had to hold fast until November, when the first frosts would freeze the ground. Then Zhukov would be able to launch his offensive, with armies that would sweep in from

north and south in a massive pincer movement, trapping Paulus exactly as he had intended.

With time running out, on October 4 Paulus attempted what he hoped would be a final offensive, with an assault on three remaining Soviet strongpoints—the tractor factory, the Barricades arms plant, and the Red October steelworks. So intense was the fighting that tanks rolled off the production line straight into battle, and workers downed tools to pick up rifles. By early November, Russian ground had been reduced to two enclaves less than 8 miles (12.8 km) long.

However, Russian reinforcements continued to arrive. A total of 122,000 soldiers struggled across the Volga to replace the 80,000 dead, while behind the lines Zhukov had 500,000 men, 900 tanks, and 1,100 planes ready for counterattack. The campaign was to be a mirror image of

Hitler's own plans, aiming for nothing less than the destruction of German forces in the south. Paulus, for his part, had little hope of reinforcements, for the forces to the rear—many of them unwilling conscripts from allied countries—had neither the spirit nor experience to withstand an all-out attack, let alone something of the size and scope that was planned.

The Germans Are Trapped

On the morning of November 19, which was bitterly cold with flurries of snow, 3,500 Russian guns opened up on Romanian troops manning the German front 100 miles (160 km) north of

Stalingrad. Within two hours, Russian infantry, backed by T-34 tanks, had overwhelmed them. The following day, the assault opened to the south of the city. Four days later, the advancing Russian spearheads met, trapping 250,000 enemy soldiers between the Volga and the Don rivers.

In his headquarters at Gumrak railway station, Paulus saw the precariousness of his position. "Army heading for disaster," he told Hitler. "It is essential to withdraw all our divisions from Stalingrad." Hitler would have none of it, relying on the boastful promise from Goering that the Luftwaffe would save the city. But Goering's plan was a fantasy. To supply the Sixth Army with over 500 tonnes of fuel, ammunition, and food every day would take 240 flights, using almost all the transport planes the Luftwaffe had. The Germans never managed one-third of the amount, and on many days they supplied nothing at all.

When an attempt to penetrate Russian lines stalled 30 miles (50 km) away in mid-December, the Sixth Army's fate was all but sealed, though they might have had one chance. Paulus could have attempted to break out and link with the German advance. But he could not bring himself to disobey Hitler, and he held grimly to a belief in rescue. Conditions meanwhile became ever more horrific, with men suffering from frostbite, dysentery, typhus, and starvation. In desperation, Paulus ordered 400 horses to be killed for food; thereafter, rations were reduced to 2 oz (50 grams) of bread and soup per day. Hitler, receiving reports of the Germans' suffering, dismissed it all as defeatism.

Soviet Victory

On December 31, the Volga locked solid with ice floes, and the first trucks rolled across to sustain the Russian defenders. Paulus, torn between loyalty to his Führer and loyalty to his troops, again appealed to Hitler. The reply he received was uncompromising: "Surrender is forbidden. Sixth Army will hold their positions to the last man and the last round." All hope for the Germans vanished. With the runway clogged by wrecks and scarred by shellholes, a few planes managed to leave, carrying with them the final letters from the doomed city. "Do not stay single for long," wrote one man to his wife. "Forget me if you can, but never forget what we endured here."

When Paulus was told there would be no more flights, he abandoned his headquarters in the railway station and set up another in a ruined department store. Thousands of wounded were stranded on the airfield; dead bodies lay everywhere, and 40,000 frostbitten, diseased, and starving men roamed or lay amidst the ruins.

On January 30, facing unprecedented catastrophe, Hitler made Paulus a field marshal, with a macabre and cynical purpose—no field marshal had ever surrendered. By tradition, a fight to the death or suicide were the only alternatives. But Paulus had been pushed beyond endurance. The next day, when a Russian tank lieutenant entered Paulus's HQ, the German field marshal stepped out and surrendered. On February 2, silence settled over the shattered city.

The Statue of Motherland and "Fight to the Death" were erected in a memorial complex to commemorate the fallen heroes of Stalingrad. The Motherland statue is the largest full-figure statue in the world, at 270 feet (82 meters) tall.

It was the end of a fearful struggle. The two sides had lost some 750,000 men. In the city itself, Russian losses were over 100,000, with German deaths amounting to 130,000. A further 100,000 shuffled off to captivity and almost certain death in Siberia. Only 5,000 Germans ever saw their homeland again.

The end meant a new beginning for Russia. Every one of the 707,000 survivors received a medal. Even as Stalingrad was saved, the Russians were driving west to reclaim the Caucasus. In conjunction with that other great victory, El Alamein, Stalingrad prepared the way for advances toward final victory.

Omaha Beach 1944

Omaha has a special place among the many battles of "The Longest Day." A number of errors of judgement combined to lead the Americans spearheading a landing force of 30,000 into an epic struggle that came to be known as "Bloody Omaha."

General Dwight D. Eisenhower (1890–1969) was Supreme Commander of the Allied Expeditionary Forces in Europe 1943-5. Born in Denison, Texas, Eisenhower had graduated from West Point Military Academy in 1915. He displayed his abilities as a strategist and co-ordinator of allied forces during the North African invasions of 1942. It was his decision to advance in line across France and Germany, but his reluctance to press on to Berlin allowed the Russians to gain an ascendancy over much of eastern Europe.

At 3 A.M. on June 6, 1944, in the pre-dawn darkness off the coast of Normandy, the U.S. troops who were to lead the invasion of Europe began to clamber from their transport ships into their landing craft. The conditions were miserable. Their 1,000 ships lay 12 miles (19 km) out to sea. A stiff 18-knot breeze whipped up a four-foot (4.8 m) swell, which made the landing craft lurch. Stumbling beneath their carapaces of equipment, many men fell, injuring themselves. Some were swept overboard.

Lead-up to Battle

Those going to the beach that would become known as "Bloody Omaha" suffered the worst. Ten of the landing craft, each carrying some 300 men, were swamped and every one of 26 artillery guns went to the bottom. It was hardly the best start for the battle that was to spearhead the reconquest of Europe.

The Allies' long-term strategy had never been in doubt. Only hours after the British had been driven off the mainland of Europe at Dunkirk in June 1940, Churchill told the House of Commons, "We shall go back!" When Russia and the U.S. were dragged into the war in 1941 and became Britain's allies, both pressed for an invasion of mainland Europe. In January 1943, the British and Americans agreed on a joint invasion the following summer.

An immense planning operation—under the supreme command of America's top general, Dwight Eisenhower—swung into action, focusing on Normandy. In the space of one year, the U.S. poured 1.5 million men into Britain, to join Britain's own forces of 1.75 million. In addition, there were 150,000 Commonwealth troops and 40,000 from occupied Europe. In vast encampments all over southern England, the troops waited for June 5: D-Day in military parlance.

The great plan, codenamed "Overlord" almost foundered. On June 4, when the troops were already in their transports, a heatwave broke. In pouring rain, Eisenhower called a 24-hour delay, and for a few hours the dreadful prospect of cancellation loomed. Then, as a break in the clouds moved in from the Atlantic early on Monday, June 5, Eisenhower gave the order to go. D-Day would be June 6.

Five thousand ships—the greatest amphibious assault ever—set sail, while above them 24,000 paratroopers and hundreds of bombers took off to secure the hinterland behind the beaches. Their destinations were five invasion beaches on a 60-mile (96-km) stretch of the Normandy coast. The first to go ashore would be the Americans, on beaches codenamed "Utah" and "Omaha." They were to be followed by the British on "Gold," "Juno," and "Sword" beaches.

Death on the Beaches

Utah proved relatively easy because the U.S. assault craft were carried by the tide to a section of beach that proved to be lightly defended.

Field Marshal Karl Rudolf Gerd von Rundstedt (1875–1953) was in commander-in-chief West, responsible for a swathe of territory from Holland to Italy. Rundstedt had become a chief of staff in the First World War and had commanded the troops that occupied the Sudetenland in 1938. He directed the Blitzkrieg across Poland and France in 1939, but was less successful in the Ukraine. Rundstedt was sacked by Hitler on 6 July 1944, but returned to command the offensive through the Ardennes in September 1944.

The view of the German defenders over the beach at Omaha.

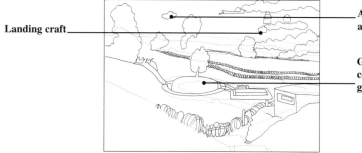

Landing craft

Amphibious tank driving around beach obstacles

German defense system of coastal artillery, machine gun posts and pillboxes

U.S. soldiers embark for Operation Overlord.

huddling around the four tracks, were a line of strongpoints: 8 big-gun emplacements, 35 pillboxes, 18 anti-tank guns, and 85 machine gun nests. Behind all this stood another line of defense, a coast road along which lay three villages to which the tracks led. All these would have to be taken if the invaders were ever to get their men and vehicles off the beach.

Omaha would at best be a tough nut, but not suicidal, according to intelligence. The troops were seasoned soldiers. Leading the assault would be three regiments of the 1st Division—known as the Big Red One—who were veterans of North Africa and Sicily. They would be fighting alongside the 29th Division's 116th This

American invaders clamber from a Coast Guard LCI into a landing barge for the last lap of the crossing to France.

German resistance crumbled, and the Americans pushed inland. Meanwhile, 10 miles (16 km) away on Omaha—a 4-mile (6.4km) sweep of sand and shingle—terrible things were happening. Omaha, the only gap in the 20 miles (32 km) of cliffs that separated Utah from the British beaches, was not a promising site for an amphibious assault. Flanked by 100-foot (30-meter) cliffs, it was backed by a steep pebble bank and dunes. Beyond these was an open 200-yard (183-meter) expanse of saltmarsh, which ended in a 150-foot (137-meter) escarpment dissected at four points by ravines, or "draws." Vehicles would have had a hard time reaching the four tracks that led inland, even without opposition.

And there would be plenty of opposition, for it was an easy beach to defend and an obvious assault point. Mined obstacles—iron frames, wooden stakes set at an angle, steel "hedgehogs" that would hole incoming craft—littered the shallows. The dunes were topped with barbed wire and a concrete wall. Anti-tank ditches crisscrossed the saltmarsh, which was well mined. From the cliffs at either end, 75mm and 88mm guns could rake the beach from behind walls 3 feet (1 meter) thick. Facing the beach, mostly

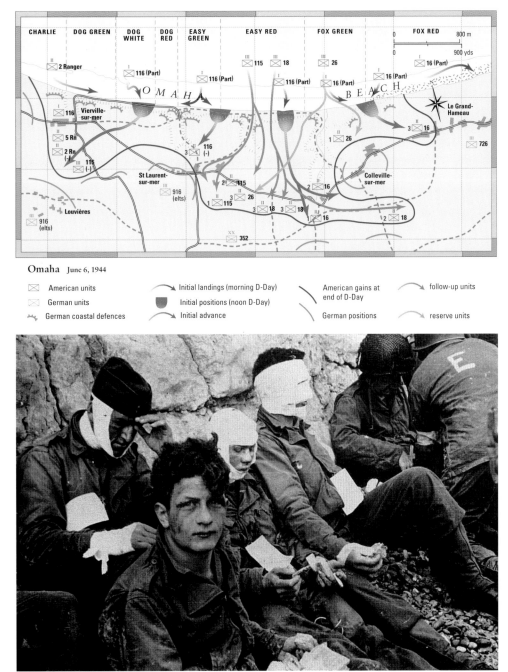

Omaha June 6, 1944

⊠ American units

⊠ German units

⋏⋏⋏ German coastal defences

→ Initial landings (morning D-Day)

◣ Initial positions (noon D-Day)

↘ Initial advance

⌒ American gains at end of D-Day

⌒ German positions

⌒ follow-up units

⌒ reserve units

Regiment. This battle-hardened force would supposedly be confronted by no more than 1,000 men of the 716th Infantry, mostly Polish or Russian conscripts who would surely show no fight-to-the-death commitment. Speed, courage, experience, overwhelming numbers, and two battalions of amphibious "DD" tanks—some 60 in all—would carry the day.

What the Allies did not know, however, was that part of Germany's 352nd Infantry Division, tough veterans of the Eastern Front, had moved up from St.-Lo several weeks before, doubling the number of defenders from four battalions to eight. By an odd coincidence, they had just completed an anti-invasion exercise and were more than ready to counter the American landing.

On top of this came the windblown, sickly voyage—and then much worse when the DD tanks were launched about four miles (6.4 km) offshore. With their canvas sides, they were supposed to float once launched. The result was nightmarish. Of the 29 tanks intended for the eastern end of the beach, 21 sank like steel coffins, taking almost all their crew with them. One was sunk by a landing craft, and two others fell victims to German guns. Only two made it to shore with the first wave of troops.

The invaders took heart from the accompanying bombardment—the salvos of rockets launched from the approaching fleet, the booms and flashes as the battleships *Texas* and *Arkansas* opened up behind them, the drone of the Eighth Air Force Fortresses above, and the crash of exploding bombs ahead. But the heavy bombers, with only brief glimpses of the ground through heavy clouds, missed their targets. Their 13,000 bombs fell uselessly on fields. And with the low clouds, the dust, and the smoke, the gunners at sea could not aim very well either.

American troops of the 3rd Battery, 16th Infantry injured while storming Omaha, await evacuation.

The bombardment killed very few of the enemy.

Ashore, the Germans watched and waited as the first wave—1,450 men in 36 landing craft—approached at 6.30 A.M., the coxswains fighting to maneuver their craft through the labyrinth of angular steel obstacles and stakes. They were almost dead in the water, making perfect targets. From the strongpoint directly in front of the lead landing craft a quarter of a mile away, came the first burst of machine gun fire. More followed. The Americans approaching in their landing craft heard the unnerving sound of bullets clanging on the steel hulls. At the same moment, howitzer shells screamed in to blast the beach with sand and flying shrapnel.

The 116th were the first out at 6.36 A.M., taking the right (western) sector. As the ramps of the first four landing craft went down, the men saw the shallows ahead whipped white by bullets. Omaha was bloody from the first, when the first men who lumbered down the ramps into waist-deep water fell in the inferno of criss-cross fire from artillery, mortars, machine guns, and rifles. Those who survived drowning and the bullets to drag themselves ashore found no shelter, and many crawled back into the scant protection of the breaking waves. Within ten minutes every officer and sergeant had been either killed or wounded. The living edged in with the rising tide, sometimes sheltering behind metal obstacles or wooden

The beachheads by the end of the first day were receiving continuous supplies and reinforcements to maintain the impetus of the landings.

stakes, hauling on their floundering companions to save them from drowning, only to see them hit and to be hit themselves. Within 20 minutes, the first men ashore, in the words of the official history, were nothing more than a "forlorn little rescue party bent upon survival."

Behind them came wave after wave of other troops, all piling into the carnage and adding to it. The current, the smoke, the noise, the maze of obstacles, and the crush of boats and corpses scrambled plans and command structures. The 270 engineers (half of whom were killed or wounded) managed to clear only one lane through the obstacles. As landing craft crowding into the single corridor dropped their ramps, men ran, jumped, and dived out to almost certain death. All along the beach, landing craft sank or exploded when they hit mines or when artillery shells blew up ammunition stacked on deck.

The only shelter on Omaha was the narrow shelf of shale and shingle a few yards wide half-way across the beach. As the troops pressed forward from the shallows on the rising tide, the beach became littered with ammunition, gas-masks, buckled radio sets, tools—all the detritus of war. The shingle shelf clogged into a solid mass of bodies, both living and dead. All momentum was lost. A terrible paralysis loomed, and General Bradley, 12 ½ miles (20 km) offshore in the U.S.S. *Augusta*, wrote later that he "gained the impression our troops had suffered an irreversible catastrophe."

The Long Agony Ends

On the beach itself, lone individuals, driven by desperation to acts of great bravery, halted the downward spiral to defeat, creating breaches in the German defenses in three places on the far left and right wings. In the center, where the remains of the 16th's 1st and 2nd Battalions lay as if crucified by bullets and shells, a lieutenant and a sergeant gallantly walked out to inspect wire barring the way. As the U.S. official history relates, the lieutenant returned and "hands on hips, looked down disgustedly at the men lying behind the shingle bank. 'Are you going to lie there and get killed, or get up and do something about it?' Nobody stirred, so the sergeant and the lieutenant got the materials and blew the wire." That encouraged the men to file through the gap and on through a minefield. Many were hit and many others fell victim to mines, but by about 10 A.M., some 300 were up the bluff and slowly fighting their way inland.

That still left most of the men trapped on the beach, which was rapidly clogging with vehicles. Something had to be done, fast, not only to lift the immediate threat, but to ensure that the U.S. troops had a secure foothold before the Germans could send reinforcements—something they were extraordinarily slow to do.

Turning Point

At 11 A.M. the tide of battle began to turn. Destroyers moved inland to within 800 yards (790 meters) of the shore, swung broadside, and delivered salvo after salvo. The 1st Division's commander, Colonel George Taylor, in a legendary incident yelled down the beach: "Two kinds of people are going to stay on this beach, the dead and those who are going to die. Now, let's get the hell out of here!" Then, as three DD tanks blasted the German emplacement ahead, he led an advance through wire and minefields. An hour and a half after landing in Taylor's wake, the 18th Infantry advanced uphill, over the plateau, and on into Colleville, where the 16th were already fighting house-to-house. Steadily, other strongpoints fell. By late afternoon, as the engineers at last cleared ways through the minefields, the first vehicles crawled off the beach along the Colleville track in support of the

The American Military Cemetery at Colleville, Omaha Beach.

infantry. As dusk approached, several units of the 115th and 116th Infantry Regiments cut their way across the second line of defense, the coast road linking the three villages behind Omaha. By nightfall, the beachhead, protecting over 30,000 men, was a patchwork of U.S.-held pockets scattered over an area 6 miles (9.6 km) long and 2 miles (3.2 km) deep.

Meanwhile, the British, with the help of a strange assortment of specialized machinery, had had an easier time of it on their three beaches. By the time darkness fell, all five beaches were secure and many of the forces had already linked to advance inland.

On Bloody Omaha, 3,000 Americans lay dead, ensuring that the battle would rank as one of the greatest tragedies of the war. Today, well-tended cemeteries, several museums and numerous memorials record the details of that day. Visitors, like armchair strategists everywhere, still debate the wisdom of the assault. But Omaha had to be taken, and there was nothing to be done about the weather, the geography, or the defenses. Omaha would have been bloody in any event.

Iwo Jima 1945

In the United States no one but a few experts had ever heard of the small island of Iwo Jima. But as Americans struggled from island to island in their advance across the Pacific, it became infamous for the way the enemy turned it into a fortress.

Before the Second World War, Iwo Jima had been nothing more than an inconsequential Japanese island in the Pacific Ocean. Only 4 miles (6.4 km) long and half that in width, it was unpopulated except for its garrison. By early 1945, however, the Japanese had turned it into a fortress, with thousands of soldiers hidden in its vast network of tunnels. Taking Iwo Jima—an important steppingstone on the way to Japan—was never going to be easy, but there was no way of knowing that it would become the bloodiest and most heroic chapter in the history of the U.S. Marine Corps.

Strategic Position

U.S. troops had been island-hopping their way toward Japan for two years. Dozens of little palm-covered isles Americans had never heard of suddenly became household names, their stories written in blood. None, though, was more crucial than Iwo Jima, with its three strategic airfields. Their capture would not only remove a menace to American shipping, but also provide an invaluable series of bases. This would allow the Americans to provide cover for their B-29 fortresses as they struck at Japan itself, and give the bombers somewhere to return to if damaged.

The Japanese had fortified the island with skill. Mount Suribachi, a 550-foot (168-meter) extinct volcano, formed a bastion at the southern end. Twenty-one thousand men had dug 11 miles (17.6 km) of tunnels and caves beneath camouflaged pillboxes, all spinning out from an underground command post with a concrete roof 10 feet (3 meters) thick. These men were prepared to die in defense of their island. Moreover, they had been ordered to hold their fire until the last possible moment in order not to reveal their positions. Thus holed up on the island, there was little the Japanese could do except wait for the blow to fall. Their strategy, under their commander Tadamichi Kuribayashi, was to lose their lives so dearly that the U.S. would sue for peace before they had a chance to attack the mainland.

Beginning on December 8, 1944, 75 days before the planned U.S. assault, bombers struck the island daily. This culminated in a three-day naval bombardment with 40,000 shells, the longest and heaviest of the Pacific War. Airstrikes included the use of a new weapon: napalm. The aerial assault destroyed 100 Japanese aircraft, but otherwise, as the Americans were to discover, it had very little effect.

On the morning of February 19, 450 ships of the US Fifth Fleet—the largest naval force yet in the Pacific theater—gathered offshore, transferring some 30,000 men into landing craft. They were under the command of Lt. General Holland M. Smith, known as "Howling Mad" Smith, both for his initials and for his ferocious temper. Smith was well qualified, for he had been in charge of marine training for four years, and had already commanded Marines in three Pacific campaigns.

The first ashore were 8,000 Marines of the 4th and 5th Marine Divisions. Under their officer

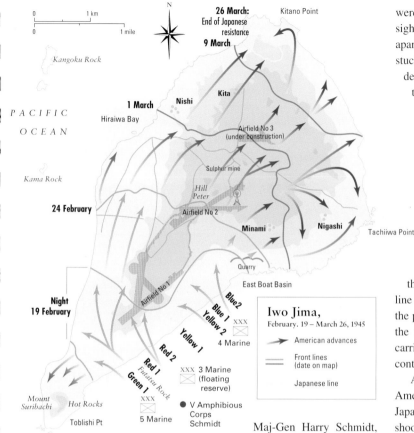

were perfect targets. The beach became a hellish sight, littered with corpses, many of them blown apart. The living sought pathetic shelter behind stuck vehicles and beneath the bodies of their dead comrades. Wounded men staggered back to the water, only to witness the first two boats carrying stretchers and stretcher-bearers blown right out of the water. Casualties who were awaiting evacuation were hit where they lay. That day, some 2,400 Americans died.

Suribachi Is Seized

Some of the Marines made progress, however. During the morning, a party of the 28th Regiment's 1st Battalion crossed the island. Others followed, strengthening the line by cutting off Mount Suribachi and opening the path to its lower slopes. The grueling fight to the summit took three days, during which the carriers and their escorts out at sea laid down a continuous barrage.

At sea, one of the hazards against which the Americans had little defense were the swarms of Japanese kamikaze planes. Almost impossible to shoot down, these human missiles were devastating in their accuracy and explosive power. The implacable kamikaze ("divine wind") pilots, named after the wind that had destroyed the invading Mongol fleet in 1281, had been in action

Maj-Gen Harry Schmidt, the Marines landed on the beaches shortly after 9 A.M. They were followed by larger craft with tanks, artillery, and bulldozers. The Marines had no warning of the hell that lay ahead. Continued bombardment meant that the landscape was shrouded in smoke and dust; the Japanese, meanwhile, held their fire. For 20 minutes, the Marines struggled ashore over two terraces of clinging volcanic ash and cinders until they were in the very lee of Mount Suribachi —and its invisible army of defenders.

Then the Japanese opened up, with a rain of artillery, mortars, and small-arms fire. With their vehicles bogged in the soft ground, the Marines

On February 19, 1945, 8,000 marines in 450 vessels race for the shore in the lee of Mt. Suribachi.

since October 1944. Now, off Iwo Jima, kamikaze attacks sank the escort carrier *Bismarck Sea*, killing 218 men, and crippled the carrier *Saratoga*. In all, almost 900 U.S. sailors were to die in the battle for Iwo Jima.

The bombardment from sea and the steady if slow advance of troops had their effect, however, and by mid-morning on February 23, the Marines had reached the top of Mount Suribachi. At 10.20 A.M., platoon leader Lt. Harold Schrier and some of his men set the Stars and Stripes flying, using a discarded water pipe as a pole. On the mountain below, Marines cheered and wept to see their flag raised high, while out at sea U.S. ships sounded their whistles. Schrier and his men then turned to the job of clearing the crater, shooting the Japanese as they sprang from their bunkers,

sweeping hiding places with flame-throwers, and sealing them off with explosives. Later, some 150 Japanese bodies were found scattered around the crater rim.

The assault produced one of the war's most famous images: the raising of "Old Glory" on the peak. But it could not have been a record of the moment, for although there was a photographer with Schrier—Sergeant Louis Lowery—a fall broke his camera. In fact, the great picture was a retake. After the crater was cleared, Associated Press photographer Joe Rosenthal arrived with another, larger flag. He was well aware that the image he sought had tremendous emotional clout —it recalled the sight that greeted Francis Scott Key when he saw the American flag still flying over the smoking Fort McHenry in 1814, the inci-

dent that inspired "The Star-Spangled Banner." Rosenthal persuaded the Marines to restage the event using the new "Old Glory," and shot a classic. Sent by seaplane to Guam and then by radiophone to the U.S., the picture was at once greeted with acclaim. President Roosevelt ordered the six flag-raisers home to share their glory, not knowing that three of them had died in subsequent fighting. The image became an icon of patriotism, to be used on stamps, in paintings, and as a model for statues, the most famous being the U.S. Marine Corps War Memorial at Arlington, Virginia.

On February 24 the fight for the rest of the island began. Tanks and artillery were of little use, for there was no room to maneuver in the difficult terrain. Every enemy position had to be taken head-on, with machine gun fire, grenades, and flame-throwers. Marines were forced to advance blind, knowing that the first they would know of the enemy would be a burst of fire or a grenade from a hole, cave, or tunnel invisible behind bushes or in a grassy bank. Each sector acquired a macabre nickname: Bloody Gorge, Meatgrinder Hill. The last was taken and lost five times before the Marines took it permanently.

Victory at a Price

Within a week, the Marines had taken a third of the island, including the main airfield. After two weeks, 82,000 men were ashore and the Americans controled all three airfields. On March 4, the first bombers made emergency landings there. Four days later, in the far southeast corner, a force of 800 Japanese staged a suicide charge in which all died. On March 11, the last main group of Japanese survivors was pinned down in a small pocket in the northwest. The final

The U.S. army magazine for April 13, 1945 featured marines on Iwo Jima a month after the island was captured.

death-defying message from General Kuribayashi came on March 21: "Have not eaten or drunk for five days, but fighting spirit is running high." He died leading a suicide charge four days later, and the fighting on Iwo Jima stopped—or almost stopped, for even the end was not quite what it seemed. A few pockets of soldiers remained, stubbornly fighting on whenever they had the chance. It was another two months before the Americans had complete control of all the island.

In five weeks of fighting, almost 7,000 Marines had been killed. Twenty-six received the U.S.'s highest award —the Medal of Honour. Admiral Nimitz said that "Among the Americans who served on Iwo Island, uncommon valor was a common virtue." As for the Japanese, the battle took the lives of nearly every one of the 21,000

soldiers involved—only 1,083 were left alive to be taken prisoner.

No one on the American side doubted that the sacrifice was worthwhile. In April, fighters based on Iwo Jima acted as escorts for a daytime bombing raid on Tokyo, and the next few months saw 2,251 landings by damaged Superfortress bombers that would otherwise have never made it to safety. This factor alone probably saved the lives of an estimated 25,000 airmen. There was one more island to be overcome—Okinawa—in a battle that was to prove even more destructive and against an enemy that showed no sign of abandoning its fight-to-the-death fanaticism. But it was the taking of Iwo Jima that guaranteed the advance towards the mainland—and to victory by the end of the summer.

Above and above left:
The shot of marines raising "Old Glory" over Mt. Suribachi created one of the war's most famous images, reproduced in the Marine Corps War Memorial at Arlington, Virginia.

BERLIN 1945

Berlin—the heart of the Third Reich and the fortress of its evil genius, Hitler—would have to fall before the war could end. It fell to the Russians, in an Armageddon that left 100,000 dead and a city in ruins.

A month after victory, the Soviet commander, Marshal Georgi Zhukov, meets General Bernard Montgomery when the Western allies entered Berlin.

On April 1, 1945, as the Russians and the Western allies approached each other across the dying remnants of the Third Reich, Stalin summoned his commanders. He posed an important question: "Who is going to take Berlin?" Two weeks later, the answer became evident. At 5 A.M. on April 16, 1945, the Red Army opened an overwhelming barrage along the River Oder. In the wake of half a million shells, rockets, and mortar bombs, 6,000 tanks drove out of their bridgeheads towards the heart of Germany. Berlin was a mere 35 miles (56 km) away.

The Allies Disagree

The final assault on Hitler's Germany might as easily have come from the west. If it had, the future of postwar Europe might well have been very different. Almost from the moment the U.S.

and Russia entered the war, the Allies had agreed that victory in Europe could only mean striking at Berlin. As the world's largest prewar city, with the fourth largest population, Berlin was the political, cultural, and industrial heart of the Nazi empire. Even before Hitler, it had been the heart of Germany, indeed the heart of all central Europe. Berlin would be the ultimate prize, and taking it would be the proof of victory.

During 1944, this determination became one that Churchill made his own. As Germany neared defeat, Churchill's distrust of the Soviet dictator Joseph Stalin had grown. Stalin, he believed, would replace Nazism by Bolshevism in the heart of Europe if he could. "Soviet Russia," he wrote later, "had become a mortal danger to the free world." For this reason, it was not only imperative to take Berlin; it was vital that the western powers—Britain, the U.S., and their allies—should seize Berlin first before the Russians got there. In June 1944, General Dwight D. Eisenhower, supreme commander of Allied forces in Europe, agreed.

But there was a hidden confusion in the policy. At the Yalta Conference in February 1945, the Allies agreed on a temporary division of the Reich into four sections, with the eastern section under Soviet administration. Berlin was to be a separate entity, also divided four ways. But the city would be isolated within the Soviet sector. What was supposed to happen if the western allies seized Berlin before the Russians? Both sides had their suspicions. Stalin feared that his

The Berlin Chancellery after the final assault.

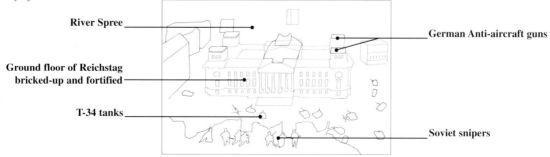

River Spree

German Anti-aircraft guns

Ground floor of Reichstag bricked-up and fortified

T-34 tanks

Soviet snipers

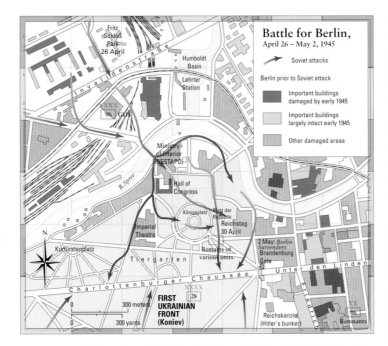

Battle for Berlin,
April 26 – May 2, 1945

→ Soviet attacks

Berlin prior to Soviet attack

Important buildings
damaged by early 1945

Important buildings
largely intact early 1945

Other damaged areas

partners—and future opponents—would simply sit tight. Churchill feared the opposite—that if the Russians got to Berlin first, they would never allow the Western allies in at all. All the more reason, then, to press on to Berlin fast.

Therefore, it came as a profound shock when Eisenhower changed his mind. He had several reasons for doing so. Firstly although the Americans and British could almost certainly beat the Russians to Berlin, they would meet extremely tough resistance from the remaining German units there. Casualties would be high. Would it not be better to let the Russians bear the brunt? Secondly, the U.S. high command had become preoccupied with reports that the Nazis planned to establish a "National Redoubt" in their homeland, the Bavarian Alps. They were anxious to send troops south to prevent such a stronghold forming. Finally, the U.S. president, Franklin Roosevelt, simply did not share Churchill's skepticism about Stalin. In April, Eisenhower's chief of staff, General Walter Bedell Smith, told a press conference that "from a purely military standpoint, Berlin does not have much significance anymore." For all these reasons, Eisenhower ordered his armies to concentrate southward on Munich.

Unwilling to provoke a rift with the Americans—who outnumbered the British forces by three to one—Churchill unhappily agreed. With German resistance collapsing, the Americans and the British found themselves on the River Elbe just 60 miles (96 km) from Berlin. There, they stopped and waited, leaving Berlin to be taken by the Russians.

Preparations for Showdown

To defend Berlin, Hitler declared it a fortress city. Teenage boys and men in their fifties were called up. As many people as possible were set to work building fortifications, trenches, strongpoints, and tank traps. Walls were covered with slogans such as: "Victory or Siberia!" Three massive defensive lines were created, stretching 200 miles (320 km) from the Baltic to the mountains of the Czech border. One million men were concentrated in the Berlin sector, with over 10,000 guns, 1,500 tanks, and 3,300 aircraft. Berlin itself was defended by 200,000 men. The city's underground railway and drains became defensive tunnels; apartment blocks were turned into fortresses; and railways and road bridges were prepared for demolition.

Formidable though this was, it was not the product of a sound mind: Hitler had not left Berlin for a month, and as the end approached he retreated into the system of bunkers 50 feet (15 meters) beneath the Chancellery, isolated from his people and his troops. Here he sank into a world of fantasy, becoming prey to terrible rages. His only release came from the presence of his vapid and undemanding mistress, Eva Braun, who was eager to participate in anything he offered, even death. With Berlin in flames from Allied air raids, Hitler's mind and body seemed to reflect the collapsing world around him. "His left arm hung slackly and his hand trembled," wrote one of his aides-de-camp. "All his movements were those of a senile man." He placed his faith in miracles and horoscopes predicting that Germany would rise again. When news came on April 12 that President Roosevelt had died, his staff declared the event a sign of divine intervention.

There would be no escape. The Russian forces on the Oder, many of them concentrated on a great bridgehead opposite Kustrin, were up to three times the size of the Nazi armies, with 2.5 million men, 42,000 guns and mortars, over 6,000 tanks, and some 8,300 aircraft. Set out in three "fronts," their generals were men of legendary

Restaging a symbolic act of victory, a Soviet soldier raises the Hammer and Sickle from a pinnacle of the Reichstag.

reputation: Georgi Zhukov, the defender of Stalingrad, and two of his closest colleagues, Konstantin Rokossovsky and Ivan Koniev.

The barrage and the advance on April 16 broke through the German defenses in two days. To the north, Rokossovsky trapped a Panzer army against the Baltic coast. In the center and south, Zhukov and Koniev's groups thrust westward, sweeping toward each other to meet in Berlin.

April 20 was Hitler's 56th birthday, and the Nazi leaders gathered for what would be the last time. Hitler had been planning to move to his summer retreat in Berchtesgaden in the Bavarian Alps, and his chiefs of staff urged him to leave while there was still time. Still, he could not believe that the end had come, and when the others left, he stayed on. The military leaders returned to their posts, and the Nazi old guard fled, including the obese Goering—Hitler's designated successor—with truckloads of booty.

The Final Battle

On April 21, Zhukov's troops broke through Berlin's outer ring of autobahns. Hitler responded by ordering General Felix Steiner's 11th Army, which was somewhere to the northwest, to break through Soviet lines. For all that day and the next, Hitler waited for rescue, but the attack never came. No one could even find Steiner. Hitler fell into a paroxysm of rage and insisted that he would stay to the end—and to the death.

Then, on April 23, Goering sent him a telegram from Bavaria suggesting that since Hitler was trapped in Berlin, he (Goering) should take over the Reich. Responding with his only means of communication—a radio transmitter suspended by balloon above the Chancellery—Hitler declared that Goering had committed treason and ordered his arrest.

Meanwhile, General Ivan Koniev was swinging in from the south. On April 24, Zhukov and Koniev's troops met to the west of Berlin and encircled the city, and two days later the final assault opened. They met fanatical resistance. SS teams ensured that no soldier left his post by shooting or hanging those who tried to defect. Civilians cowered in their cellars, awaiting the end. On April 25, U.S. and Russian troops met at Torgau on the Elbe, some 75 miles (120 km) south of Berlin. Hitler was cut off in Berlin.

The next day, shells began to land on the Chancellery itself, and those in the bunker could hear the thud of explosions. The Germans in the city now held only a narrow east–west corridor less than 3 miles (4.8 km) wide and 10 miles (16 km) long. Soon the Russians had broken the corridor into three pockets, and were fighting their way to the parliament building (the Reichstag), through the zoo park (Tiergarten).

Hitler at last saw that the end had come. Another order for counterattack led to nothing, for the armies Hitler thought he commanded were either vanquished or fleeing. On the 28th, in a bizarre ritual, he married Eva Braun as a reward for her 12 years of subservient loyalty. He concluding with a speech anticipating his death. Then, late into the night, he dictated his will.

Acting the good father in happier times, the Nazi propaganda minister Josef Goebbels parades four of his children for the camera. The day before Berlin fell, he ordered all six killed by injection and then had himself and his wife shot through the head.

End of the Third Reich

Early on April 30, the Russians took the Gestapo building near the Reichstag and then started bombarding the Reichstag itself. The German parliament, a huge nineteenth-century building with a Neo-classical portico and pillars, was the very heart of Nazism—the place set on fire by the Nazis to provide an excuse for their seizure of power in 1933, and the place where Hitler had made his most notorious speeches. The Reichstag had now been turned into a fortress, with its doors and windows bricked up, leaving only firing slits. Its 5,000 defenders—men of the SS, the Hitler Youth, and the Volkssturm (Home Guard)—turned every room, corridor, and staircase into a battleground. On the evening of the 30th, two Red Army sergeants hoisted the red flag from one of the portico's pinnacles, but the room-by-room battles continued for another two days, during which half the defendants died.

By the time the Reichstag was taken, Hitler was already dead. He had his papers burned and his favorite dog, Blondi, poisoned. After lunch on the 30th, with the Russians closing in from the Tiergarten and only a block from the Chancellery, he summoned Eva. The two said their farewells to two members of the inner circle of Nazis: The propaganda minister Josef Goebbels and Hitler's secretary, Martin Bormann. Then, at about 3.30 P.M., a shot was heard. Eva had taken cyanide, and Hitler had shot himself. Their bodies were taken outside and burned, as shells exploded nearby—part of a bombardment that obliterated the remains before they could be retrieved and identified by Allied soldiers.

On May 1, Goebbels and Bormann sent General Hans Krebs to try to negotiate a ceasefire. The Russians demanded unconditional surrender, but Goebbels and Bormann rejected the idea and the attacks resumed. The bunker was set on fire and its defenders—some 500 SS men—fled. Later, Goebbels committed suicide with his wife and six children, and Bormann vanished, probably killed.

Early on May 2, Berlin's battle commandant made a radio broadcast declaring surrender, and that afternoon the fighting died down as the surviving German soldiers laid down their arms. Six days later, the local surrender became national.

Berlin lay in ruins. William Shirer, a war correspondent and author, described the view of the city from the air as "a great wilderness of debris dotted with roofless burned out buildings that look like little mouse traps with low autumn sun

100,000 civilians had died in battle. Marauding Red soldiers went on an orgy of destruction, pillage, and rape. A single Berlin hospital treated 230 rape victims in one day. The Russian troops had been told that everything movable was lawful booty, so they took what they could: Clothing, watches, pens, furniture, and appliances. Berliners were reduced to destitution. There were even rumors of cannibalism.

Only in July, when the Americans, British, and

Refugees wander through the streets of Berlin, in which food and shelter were at a premium.

shining through the spaces where windows had been. Most of the little streets I knew gone, erased off the map, railroad stations . . . gaunt shells, the imperial palace of the Kaisers—roofless, some of its wings pulverized."

For Berliners, this was the worst of times. Some 100,000 soldiers and perhaps another

French arrived to take control of their sectors of the city, did a semblance of normalcy begin to return. But by then Berlin was firmly fixed within that part of Germany that would become East Germany. It was not until the collapse of Communism in 1989 that Berlin would regain its historic place at the heart of a reunified country.

KHE SANH 1968

During the 77-day siege of Khe Sanh, the fate of U.S. forces in Vietnam seemed to hang in the balance. To the world, it looked as if the U.S. had been drawn into a trap from which there was no escape. There was indeed a trap—but it was not Khe Sanh.

For a few weeks in 1968, almost every ambitious young journalist and photographer in Vietnam wanted to brave a trip into Khe Sanh. Some 6,000 Marines were trapped in a remote jungle base, surrounded by 20,000 North Vietnamese troops. They had been forced by the enemy artillery to take temporary shelter in bunkers sandbagged for their protection.

For a while, the Marines' plight looked like a preliminary to one of the greatest military disasters ever to engulf U.S. armed forces. But as time passed, it became evident that Khe Sanh was only part of a much wider plan that had been devised by the North Vietnamese.

A Disaster in the Making

Although Khe Sanh was part of the much wider disaster of the war as a whole, for the Vietnamese even the war was part of a far greater context. For them, it was the last chapter in a saga that stretched back to before the Second World War, when nationalists and communists opposed French colonial rule. After 1945, the French ruled for nine years before losing their colony at the battle of Dien Bien Phu, a victory masterminded by the Communist leader Ho Chi Minh and his commander, Vo Nguyen Giap.

At the peace conference that followed in Geneva, Vietnam was divided into the communist north and the nationalist south, pending elections that would reunify the country. The division, which ran along the 17th parallel, was declared a Demilitarized Zone, or "DMZ." The South, fearing an electoral loss to the communists, declared a republic. The North covertly backed insurgents known as the Viet Cong ("Vietnamese Communists") in the South. The United States, nervous of the spread of what they saw as a unified communist empire from eastern Europe to Peking, aided the southern regime.

In the early 1960s, the Viet Cong were increasingly supplied with arms and provisions from the North, and the dictatorial and corrupt southern regime, under Ngo Dinh Diem, proved mostly

Marines defending Khe Sanh fire a M-101 105mm howitzer. This weapon could be airlifted into position by helicopter. An eight-man crew could deliver 100 rounds an hour over a range of 6 miles (9.6km).

The scene of the battle today is now farmland, although much is still dangerous because of unexploded bombs.

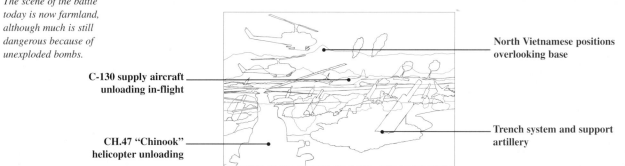

North Vietnamese positions overlooking base

C-130 supply aircraft unloading in-flight

Trench system and support artillery

CH.47 "Chinook" helicopter unloading

ineffective up against the communist guerrillas.

Vietnam was ideal terrain for guerrillas, with jungle-covered mountains stretching from the DMZ to Saigon. The people were concentrated on the coast, leaving the inland jungles and mountains relatively unpopulated. South of Saigon, the delta of the Mekong river offered a maze of backwaters and swamps. And Vietnam's western boundaries ran for 625 miles (1,000 km) through the inaccessible jungles of Laos and Cambodia, easily infiltrated from the north along the so-called Ho Chi Minh Trail.

The U.S. president, Lyndon Johnson, was faced with the possibility of a communist victory, which would result in the collapse of U.S. policy in southeast Asia and the humiliating evacuation of its 20,000 troops based in South Vietnam. Steadily, the war came to be seen as a testing ground for two ideologies, communist and capitalist. From 1964, the war became one of the U.S. against North Vietnam. In 1965, the U.S. began

bombing the North, while the North received supplies from China and the Soviet Union.

The ideologies were reflected by two opposing military strategies: Guerrillas versus regulars, manpower against machines. American strategy relied on technological superiority, with forces engaged both in "search and destroy" missions and in the creation of bases from which massive firepower could be deployed. By late 1967, American forces had reached half a million, costs were $30 billion a year, and casualties were mounting. Johnson was coming up for re-election and needed at least to avoid humiliation. It was within this pressured context that the siege of Khe Sanh developed.

The Siege in the Jungle

Khe Sanh, a quiet mountain village 15 miles (25 km) south of the DMZ, was on the road leading west from the coast and lay 6 miles (9.6 km) short

Armed helicopters at Khe Sanh wait for their next "search and destroy" mission.

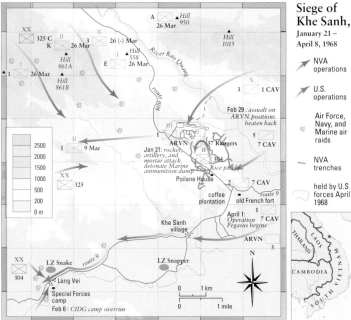

Siege of Khe Sanh,
January 21 –
April 8, 1968

↗ NVA operations

↗ U.S. operations

✳ Air Force, Navy, and Marine air raids

— NVA trenches

held by U.S forces April 1968

of the Laotian border. It thus straddled a route favored by the North Vietnamese as they infiltrated from the north via the Ho Chi Minh Trail. On this small plateau overlooked by jungle-clad hills, the French had built an airstrip. The U.S. Special Forces already had a camp there, and in September 1966, General William Westmoreland, the U.S. commander, decided to reinforce it. Besides depriving the North Vietnamese of an infiltration route, Westmoreland thought it might be useful one day to have a base from which the Ho Chi Minh Trail could be cut, if the U.S. ever decided to extend the war across the border.

But there were two deeper reasons for building up the base. First, it would attract thousands of enemy troops who would be pulverized by American firepower. Secondly, Khe Sanh was to be part of a series of strongpoints covered by "Long Toms," 175mm guns that could fire a 147-pound (64 kg) shell 20 miles (32 km)—a policy that would force the enemy into corridors that would make them into easy targets.

To hold and strengthen Khe Sanh, Westmoreland sent in two battalions of Marines

A U.S. Air Force C-130 Hercules transporter roars into Khe Sanh, deploying a parachute to whip supplies out as the plane touches down, allowing it to take off again before it is hit.

in April 1967. Their first task was to seize the nearby hills and ridges. Here, the North Vietnamese had dug themselves in over several months, preparing pole-and-earth bunkers that only direct hits with a bomb could penetrate. Protected from preliminary air raids and almost invisible in their foxholes, they mauled the attacking Marines brutally. In two and a half weeks of fighting, some 1,800 U.S. Marines engaged North Vietnamese troops in a bitter fight for three hills overlooking the airfield. There was no defeat, but no victory either. The Vietnamese simply slipped away to fight another day, and the Marines lost 155 men, with 425 wounded—their worst losses for any battle to date. They were left with two of the hills, while a third—known as Hill 881 North—was considered to be too far from the base to be held securely.

It seemed to many—Westmoreland himself made the connection—that the North Vietnamese

were planning to repeat their crushing victory at Dien Bien Phu. The comparison appalled Johnson, who wrung from Westmoreland a formal commitment that Khe Sanh would not fall. He promised this was to be a Dien Bien Phu in reverse, the bastion against which the Viet Cong and North Vietnamese would break themselves.

Determined to consolidate, the U.S. flew in reinforcements—three Marine battalions, making a total of 6,680 men by early 1968—when the fog, clouds, and rain of the monsoon shrouded the runway. At the same time, the North Vietnamese built up their forces in the forested hills to two infantry divisions of some 20,000 men.

Early on January 21, 1968, the battle proper opened. At 5.30 A.M. artillery shells, 122mm rockets and mortars rained on to the airstrip from Hill 881 North. One shell hit a cache of tear gas, sending choking clouds across the Marine bunkers. Another struck an ammunition dump and detonated 1,500 tons of explosives.

In response, the U.S. began massive airstrikes. Every three hours round the clock, six B-52s from Strategic Air Command based on the Pacific

island of Guam "carpet-bombed" a "box" of jungle from 6 miles (9.6 km) above the cloud cover. Each B-52 could unload over 40 500-lb (227-kg) bombs. In the course of the battle, the U.S. would drop the equivalent of five Hiroshima-type bombs on the hills around Khe Sanh. In between these raids, fighter-bombers struck about every five minutes dive-bombing through the lowering clouds with 750-, 1,000-, and 2,000-lb (340-, 454-, and 908-kg) bombs. Flights of jets were stacked up as high as 36,000 feet (10,972 meters), awaiting their turn to reduce further the cratered forest. Meanwhile, 46 howitzers sandbagged into the base and 175mm cannons in camps 5 miles (8 km) to the east added to the assault.

Re-Supply

Relief planes braved flak and rockets from the jungle to parachute in supplies. Transports that were often forced below 500 feet (152 meters) by monsoon clouds roared in through hails of machine-gun fire with food, ammunition, and medics. The ubiquitous Bell UH-1 Huey helicopters landed journalists by the score, eager to cover the bravery of the grimy, haggard troops. Marines sheltered in trenches from the incoming mortars. At night, the North Vietnamese crept up to the perimeter fences to terrorize the occupants with machine-guns, grenades, and satchel bombs.

As week followed week, Western media awaited the possible capture of the base, a loss that would have immense political and military repercussions. In the Situation Room in the basement of the White House, President Johnson had a table-top model of Khe Sanh built so that he could follow the battle in detail.

At the end of January—the time of the Buddhist New Year (Tet)—the crisis escalated seriously. At

Marines shelter in a trench. Recruits soon learned to tell "incoming" mortars from "outgoing."

this traditional time of peace, Westmoreland had declared a cease-fire everywhere except around Khe Sanh, assuming that his enemies would observe it as well. Unfortunately for him Giap, a military genius who had once earned his living teaching history in Hanoi, had other ideas. As the siege of Khe Sanh intensified, he was preparing the most devastating assault yet aimed at the heartland of South Vietnam.

Later, it became clear that Khe Sanh was never intended to be another Dien Bien Phu. Giap was perfectly well aware of his former strength and present weakness: In 1954 his forces had out-numbered the French; the French could not be resupplied by air; and the position was now reversed. He could never defeat the Americans in a straight fight. What he wanted was to create a long-lasting distraction, so the siege was always conducted on Giap's terms. Khe Sanh was not subjected to an all-out assault. Though some 200 Marines were to die in Khe Sanh, this loss was small compared to the thousands lost by the Vietnamese. The flak, rockets, and mortars were not enough to prevent resupplies from arriving—but they were enough to tie down thousands of U.S. troops, bombers and transports, to hypnotize U.S. military and political leaders, to seize the attention of the Western press, and to turn all attention away from the real attack, timed for the Buddhist New Year (Tet).

The attack, soon known as the Tet Offensive, was intended to spark a general uprising in the South. In a campaign of staggering imagination and scope, tens of thousands of Viet Cong and North Vietnamese attacked scores of American and South Vietnamese targets: 6,000 Viet Cong moved into Saigon, and on January 30, they even assaulted the U.S. Embassy, forcing the ambassador, Elsworth Bunker, to flee the building in his pajamas. Practically the only place that remained unaffected was Khe Sanh itself, where the bombardment remained exactly the same.

A CH-53 Sea Stallion helicopter brings in supplies to beleaguered Khe Sanh

For 77 days, the siege of Khe Sanh continued. Relief, in an operation codenamed "Pegasus", came in April, as the 1st U.S. Air Cavalry and a South Vietnamese battalion worked their way up from the south and the 1st Marines from the east. On April 6, when most North Vietnamese had been withdrawn, the Air Cavalry cut through to bring the siege to an end. A clash on Easter Sunday, April 14, drove the remaining North Vietnamese from Hill 881 North. The Tet Offensive did not spark revolution as the North Vietnamese had hoped. The excesses of the Viet Cong, who murdered some 3,000 officials, guaranteed popular opposition. Nor was it a military victory for Giap —his forces lost 30,000.

But it struck a fatal psychological blow to the Americans. It disoriented their military response, driving them into paradox and impasse. Westmoreland proclaimed that the Tet Offensive was a diversion designed to attract attention away from Khe Sanh. Unable to distinguish friend from foe, the Americans turned to random destruction. As a major said after strikes on Ben Tre left the place a ruin: "It became necessary to destroy the town in order to save it." Westmoreland was "kicked upstairs" as army chief of staff—in effect fired. The bombing of North Vietnam was suspended. At home the country was divided, and Johnson did not stand for re-election. In May, peace talks opened. It took another seven years for America to concede defeat, but after Khe Sanh and the Tet Offensive, few Americans believed anymore that the war could be won.

DESERT STORM

The military operation that took Kuwait back from the invading Iraqis was the greatest military operation since the invasion of Normandy in 1944. Weight of arms triumphed, with astonishing speed and few casualties—yet with far less than total victory.

Saddam Hussein, the Iraqi dictator, sacrificed his country on the altar of his own ego. In defeat, he retained power and remained in bloody control of his shattered country.

The Iraqi invasion of Kuwait in 1990–1 astonished the world three times over. The first surprise was the invasion itself, when at 2 A.M. local time on August 2, 1990, Iraqi forces thrust across their southern border into Kuwait. The response was as astonishing as the invasion. Iraqi forces were thrown back by the greatest joint operation since the Second World War. Since the Iraqi dictator Saddam Hussein promised "the mother of all battles", and Western leaders believed him, the events that then unfolded—the assault known as Desert Storm—produced the third great surprise.

A Long Standing Dispute

The world should not have been surprised by the invasion, for the crisis had been brewing for years. Saddam had long wanted to seize Kuwait, which had been administered with Iraq until the breakup of the Ottoman Empire after the First World War. It was therefore in effect a Western artifact, with no older historical "right" to exist. But he was inspired less by history than by Kuwait's oil, worth $22 billion a year. He was in dire need of such help, for in 1988 the end of an eight-year war with Iran had left his country bankrupt. A declining economy meant rising unrest. To have Kuwait would be a welcome economic and political boost

In early 1990, Saddam's reckless unpredictability was revealed by his execution of a British journalist, Farzad Bazoft, on flimsy charges of

spying and by the revelation of a plot to import a "supergun" that would shell the real enemy: Israel. Yet Western nations urged moderation, and Saddam became convinced that an invasion would attract nothing more than verbal condemnation. Besides, there was nothing much anyone could do. His forces— a million men, 6,000 tanks and 600 planes—outnumbered those of his neighbors, and the nearest substantial U.S. force was in Germany. In mid-July, he began to mass troops along the Kuwaiti border.

Right until the last moment, Western leaders clung to the hope that Saddam was saber-rattling, or would at most seize disputed border areas. By midday on August 2, they knew better. An erratic, ambitious, and vengeful dictator was in control of one-fifth of the world's oil. Moreover, advancing at that speed, the Iraqis might be tempted to drive right on into Saudi Arabia, or spread the war to Israel. In hours, a local dispute had become a major global crisis.

It was the U.S. that seized the initiative to retain its influence over Middle Eastern oil and to assert its self-proclaimed role as champion of the "free world." On the night of the invasion, U.S. leaders thrashed out a response, then bludgeoned the U.N. into action. A series of resolutions condemned Iraq, then froze Iraqi assets. Allies were consulted to weld together what came to be called the "Coalition." It was crucial that Arab nations be on board, or American involvement would seem like Big-Brother interference. The Arabs wavered, but two days later the Arab League

Desert Storm's commander, H. Norman Schwarzkopf, was the "most theatrical American in uniform since Douglas MacArthur", in the words of one historian.

An air attack on Baghdad aimed at depriving Iraq of its defenses by destroying its command centers.

states voted 14-7 to condemn Iraq's invasion. Finally came direct action, after more delicate diplomacy. Iraq had been a Soviet client-state, and for American troops to deploy in Muslim territory might alienate the Arab people. The next U.N. Resolution (661) imposed economic sanctions to be backed by American forces "at the request of Saudi Arabia." Finally, on November 29, Resolution 678 authorized member states to use "all necessary means" to force Iraqi withdrawal. The deadline was January 15, 1991.

Saddam had only two possible options: compliance or defiance. He chose the latter.

The Buildup

Meanwhile, the U.S. had adapted longstanding plans to counter a threat from the former Soviet Union or Iran. The buildup was commanded by General H. Norman Schwarzkopf, a burly man with a fondness for equating military maneuvers with American football plays. He answered to the President George Bush, Secretary of Defense Dick Cheney, and Chairman of the Joint Chiefs of Staff General Colin Powell. Schwarzkopf wanted to move fast, using combat troops and fighter planes to secure Saudi bases and preempt a possible Iraqi strike. Then would come the real heavyweight: the support crews, the hardware, and the mobilized reserves. However, this operation intestinal infection. At Al Jubail, Marines sweated for 10 days in 140°F (60°F) while they waited to unload. Finally, on August 25, the first 15,000 men—with 123 tanks, 425 artillery pieces, and 124 aircraft rolled north to the Saudi-Kuwaiti border.

Still more tanks, armored personnel carriers, and heavy artillery were needed. These would all have to land fully armed and fueled, ready for action. Speed was vital to create overwhelming force and to finish the war before high summer in March would halt the action. The computers said it would take two weeks to get supplyships and their contents to the Gulf. In fact, it took 6–16 weeks, with hundreds of bureaucrats fighting to conquer logistical breakdowns. Then there were

A British Tornado GR1. Of Britain's 100 aircraft in the Gulf, 45 were Tornados. They dropped over 100 JP-233 runway-cratering bombs, and lost five machines in combat.

the troops of other nations to coordinate: 35,000 Egyptians, 1,200 Moroccans, 19,000 Syrians, 14,000 French, 11,500 British, and others from Kuwait, Saudi Arabia, Oman, and Qatar.

So far, the war aim was to contain Saddam. Only in mid-October did the war enter another stage— a planned offensive to push Saddam out. This would be a formidable task, or so everyone thought. The ground troops would face oil-filled trenches, barbed wire, artillery, half a million troops, and fast-moving armored formations of the supposedly elite Republican Guard. Schwarzkopf's "nightmare scenario" derived from American experience in Vietnam—a bloody war of attrition in which chemical weapons

An F-117 Lockheed Stealth fighter, one of 40 recently introduced into service. The plane, invisible to radar, carries 2,000-pound (607 kg) laser-guided bombs of pinpoint accuracy.

would take months, leaving the combat forces horribly exposed if Saddam chose to attack.

On August 7 and 8, 48 F-15C Eagles made the 16-hour flight from the U.S. (with six in-air refuellings), to land at the Coalition's main base, Dhahran, which had been built with U.S. assistance in the 1980s. Coalition fixed-wings now numbered 300, and rose to over 1,000 within a month. It was almost certainly this factor that deterred Saddam from a further advance.

Gigantic Lockheed C-5 and C-141B transporters followed with the first troops, the 2,300 men of Ready Brigade, 82nd Airborne, with their Humvees (HMMWVs, which stands for High Mobility Multi-Purpose Wheeled Vehicles—latter-day jeeps) and light tanks. Meanwhile, seven U.S. warships in the Indian Ocean headed for the Saudi port of Al Jubail.

The buildup rapidly ran aground on reefs of complex and untried logistics. For instance, since the Catering Corps had been disbanded after Vietnam, the men had to survive on their MREs (Meals Ready to Eat), resulting in 3,000 cases of

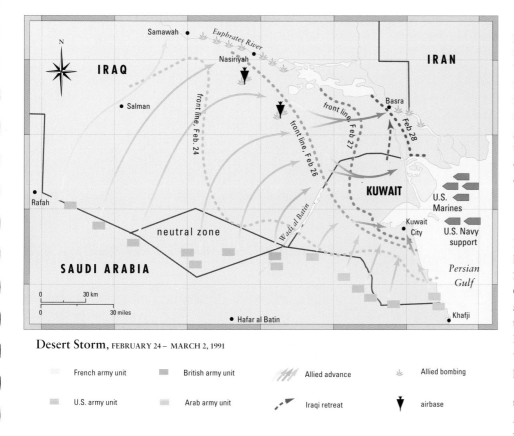

Desert Storm, FEBRUARY 24 – MARCH 2, 1991

French army unit	British army unit	Allied advance	Allied bombing
U.S. army unit	Arab army unit	Iraqi retreat	airbase

On November 10, Schwarzkopf revealed his plan, code-named "Desert Storm." "Okay," he said to his senior staff, showing them a map. "This is what I wanna do. Now you think about this and come back and tell me how I'm gonna do it." His audience gasped. The arrows on his map showed a vast outflanking maneuver that would go around Iraq's defenses, through Iraq , and trap the Iraqi forces in a pincer between two corps, co-ordinating some 270,000 men and 78,000 vehicles simultaneously along just two roads.

The "Mother of All Battles"

But the ground war would begin only after Iraq had been undermined by air raids. These started 24 hours after the deadline expired, when the Coalition had 2,430 planes—outnumbering Iraqi air power fourfold, and totally outclassing it in technology. The U.S., for instance, had several Lockheed F-117As ("stealth bombers"), which were invisible to radar and could deliver 4,000 pounds (1,814 kg) of laser-guided bombs. An F-117A's 2,000-pound (907 kg) bomb could penetrate 16 feet (5 meters) of reinforced concrete. Airborne radars could detect a single moving vehicle at 115 miles (184km). Weapons included "smart" bombs that could enter the window of a target building, the 7-ton Dairy Cutter that could flatten every standing object within a quarter of a

would erode all resistance. Casualty predictions ranged from 10,000 to 100,000. Since the Coalition was outnumbered, Schwarzkopf had to play his main card: technical superiority.

Schwarzkopf asked for yet more troops, doubling the ground forces to 400,000. Then came more hardware. Britain and the U.S. responded by stripping their bases in Germany, using some 100,000 vehicles to gather the men and equipment. At last, the supplies built up during the Cold War found a use. The ammunition alone—weighing 40,000 tons—demanded 2,200 trucks. In all, more equipment was moved from Europe to the Gulf than was stored by the U.S. for the invasion of Europe in 1944.

An amphibious assault ship alongside U.S.S. Nassau; *two of the 60 U.S. ships deployed in support of the allied ground operation.*

mile (400 meters), and cruise missiles pro-grammed with city street maps. All these were coordinated with reconnaissance satellites. Iraq would be left without a brain, before its body was ever assaulted by ground forces.

Within minutes of the start of the air war on January 16, stealth planes and cruise missiles knocked out Iraqi radar, leaving the country blind. Thereafter, the Coalition planes and mis-siles had little to stop them. The BBC's John Simpson watched astounded as a cruise missile tracked a street across the front of his hotel, turned at the corner, and found its target. Some 200 missiles removed buildings with pinpoint accuracy. By mid-February, 27 of 36 major bridges were down, one of them—as Schwarzkopf revealed to the media on video—"busted" with just a single missile. The Iraqi supply system ceased to exist, and the troops were reduced to ragged and demoralized units, terrorized by 25,700 tons of explosives dropped in 1,624 carpet-bombing sorties. The fireball from one Daisy Cutter—dropped after a three-day humanitarian warning to Iraqi troops—was

heard and seen over 100 miles (160 km) away in Al Jubail. Of 4,000 Iraqi tanks in Kuwait, 1,300 were destroyed.

One scare was created by the 86 Scud missiles fired by Iraq, because it was feared they could drop chemical or biological warheads on Israeli and on Coalition troops. As it turned out, they were inaccurate weapons, and nothing but a petty—if high profile—response. But their very use forced an extension of the air war over Iraq by a week, as up to 200 sorties a day tried—and failed—to find the launchers and destroy them.

Once Iraq had been blinded, the ground build-up could go ahead, with every hope of preserving secrecy. Forces were to be in four groupings along a 270-mile (432-km) front. While diver-sionary exercises set out to convince the Iraqis that the attack would come from the sea or the south, heavy road transporters were bought and hired wherever they could be found—4,000 in all, many of them near collapse. The convoys of men and supplies turned the quickly wrecked roads into a war zone of their own, leaving the desert littered with broken-down vehicles.

On February 22, Bush offered Saddam a final chance to withdraw. Saddam promised the

American troops advance past a burning oil field on the way north to the Iraqi border.

A British soldier moves forward during a ground assault.

Coalition troops would "tumble into the great crater of death," and stood firm.

The next day, the ground forces went in. Within hours, they discovered that American intelligence had made a fundamental error: The enemy divisions that existed on the computers did not match those on the ground, where the troops were depleted, battle-weary, and demoralized. On the Saudi-Kuwaiti border, bulldozers filled in flaming trenches that proved to be only a couple of yards wide. Tanks swept over the defenses with ease and struck out for Kuwait City. On the left, the "Screaming Eagles" of the 101st Airborne launched the largest air-mobile operation ever, using 300 helicopters to establish a base 70 miles (112 km) inside Iraq. Infantry and armored cavalry followed within a day, on a schedule accelerated by the lack of Iraqi resistance. Even in sandstorms, the Coalition vehicles could move on, checking their position and direction by GPS (global positioning system).

The feared Iraqi response never came. When Iraqi tanks fought back, they quickly fell victim to Coalition armor and artillery. The 24th Infantry approached Talil airfield south of the Euphrates Valley through 60 miles (96 km) of Iraqi territory without seeing a single Iraqi soldier. By February 25, the Coalition had 25,000 prisoners. The number of Iraqi soldiers trying to surrender slowed the advance more effectively than the fighting, and Coalition troops were more at risk from their own side than the enemy—nine out of a total of 16 British soldiers killed were victims of "friendly fire" incidents. Late on February 26, a brigade of 57 T-72 tanks fleeing north ran into the U.S. Victory Division, and every Iraqi tank was destroyed. By the end of February 27, the Coalition was in Kuwait and had achieved its objectives. "The mother of all battles" was less of a battle than a victory march.

The final phase turned into a massacre as American aircraft caught Iraqi troops on the Mutla Ridge north of Basra and turned the road into what the media termed the "Highway of Hell." With ground units closing their escape route, hundreds of Iraqis died, and more fled as the planes turned their 1,000 tanks and trucks to flaming scrap. Because media coverage revealed the extent of this "turkey shoot," public revulsion was a major factor in calling a halt. At 8 A.M. on February 28, the Coalition advance halted, allowing 700 tanks and 1,400 armored personnel carriers to escape.

That was the end of the "100 Hours War." All the predictions of dire losses had relied on Saddam's misleading boasts. Iraq lost at least 25,000 men and was left ruined. Total Coalition losses were 150 dead, 75 of whom were American; 28 died in one Scud attack on Dhahran. Saddam's forces had vanished, leaving only a terrible memento—clouds of choking smoke from over 600 oil wells deliberately set on fire. (It took 10 months to extinguish them.)

Never had a battle so powerfully exemplified the prime elements of great victories: drive, surprise, and overwhelming force.

The road to Baghdad, littered with the wreckage of Iraqi vehicles, became known as the Highway of Death.

INDEX

Page numbers in *italics* refer to captions and illustrations

CREDITS